YOUR AUTHENTIC
IDENTITY

"If anyone is in Christ, he is a new creation..."

JASON ANDERSON

Jason and Kelli Anderson are Lead Pastors at The Living Word Bible Church

www.livingwordonline.org

Title ID: Discovering Your Authentic Identity
ISBN-13: 978-1984182524

DISCOVERING
YOUR AUTHENTIC
IDENTITY

God has made you perfect, wonderful, magnificent, and full of splendor. But, have you ever wondered why you are still struggling in that one area, after years of applying every possible principle and check list that there is? Is it possible you are just always going to struggle in that same area? And, are you tired of it? We carry within each of us the desire to grow and change. We strive for the fears, worries, addictions, past, and emotional defeats all to be healed. We have a problem though. The reason there hasn't been great relief is because we have been going about this wrong. God says He made us brand new. Why am I trying to fix the old? In DISCOVERING YOUR AUTHENTIC IDENTITY, Jason Anderson takes you through the scripture, and teaches simple concepts that will have you discovering who you were created to be; the authentic and perfect you.

CONTENTS

DEDICATION AND ACKNOWLEDGEMENT

To Christian, Katy, Mathew, and Logan. Never has a father been more proud of who his children have become.

DISCOVERING
YOUR AUTHENTIC
IDENTITY

Chapter One
Conformed to the Likeness of the Son

Romans 8:28-29 (NET) *And we know that all things work together for good for those who love God, who are called according to his purpose, because those whom he foreknew he also predestined to be conformed to the image of his Son, that his Son would be the firstborn among many brothers and sisters.*

God knew you before you knew yourself. This means He knows you better than you know yourself. God also predestined you. He foreknew you and He planned you to be conformed. You might ask, "Conformed to what?" To be conformed into the likeness and image of His Son, Jesus. As a believer, you are conformed into Jesus' likeness. Romans 12:2 (NET) says it like this: "*Do not be conformed to this present world, but be transformed by the renewing of your mind.*" What is God trying to accomplish? God has conformed you to Christ, because that's who you were created to be when you were born again. The greatest you has been transformed.

Here's the problem. Most Christians are trying to change themselves to become more Christ like. They have taken the sinful nature and started making adjustments to try and make it look prettier. Make-up, do the hair, maybe a whole new wardrobe. But the *sinful nature **is being corrupted** by* *deceitful desires*, (Ephesians 4:22 NIV) whatever will you do? I know, try harder. Stop having low self-esteem, stop that addiction, and quit thinking about that nasty stuff. There, all better? Oops, fell off the wagon, try harder next time. Christians are trying to fix the old, when actually the old is just better off left in the grave where he belongs. The old you is not you. The old you was never you. The Bible says the old you was crucified in Christ. We are to put off the old self... and according to Ephesians 4:24 (NIV) *put on the new self, created to be like God in true righteousness and holiness.* The new you is complete in Christ. Complete. Wait, what? Yeah, the reason you struggle is because you have probably followed the wrong road in your attempt grow. You've worked so hard, alas, only to find out it didn't really work. Are you ready for a clearer path to your identity? I have a surprise for you. The person who makes mistakes and feels quite like a failure, rejected and condemned, yeah, that's not actually you. You're operating out of the old self again. It's a habit. I know. Do I have your attention now? Be patient, the answers are coming.

People are all trying to find themselves. Then we think, "Wait, in this book am I going to lose who I truly am as I recognize my conformed identity?" You're not going to lose yourself; you're going to find yourself. In this book, we are going to teach you how to find yourself *in Christ*, as opposed to finding yourself by *backpacking across Europe*. Everyone is off trying to find out who they are. "I just want to discover who I am." We all do. But how do you accomplish that? How you approach your goal matters. You will either find yourself successful in reaching the goal, or waste a great deal of time heading in the wrong direction.

In this book, we are on an adventure discovering who you are, but we are going to do it differently than everyone else. We are going to discover who we are through Christ. Sometimes we are concerned with being transformed or conformed, because it doesn't sound like we will be authentic. Truth be told, God's goal is to get you back to exactly who you were created to be when you were spiritually born, not the abused and tragedy-scarred person that looks at you in the mirror. There is no need to worry that you will have to let go of who you are. You're not letting go of who you are. On the contrary, you're discovering who you really are. In this, the scars and brokenness are attached to the old you. Who you thought you were *is not* actually who you are.

For instance, a broken heart changes how you respond in your future relationships. A restored heart returns you to the authentic you, as opposed to the damaged you. This is why God *has made* us new. You have been reborn! When we learn how to operate in our true identity, the crisis and storms of our life no longer impact our identity. That is, when Jesus went through betrayal and crucifixion, His character stayed true, it didn't impact who He is. He continued to operate in love and forgiveness. When we go through betrayal, it changes how we act, how we talk, and how we feel in that moment, and often into the future. We find out what is in us when we get kicked, we can see it as it comes blurting out. As it turns out, when Jesus got kicked, love and forgiveness came out.

When you become born again, God says, "I predestined you to be conformed to the likeness of my Son, Jesus." At that moment we are made new. Conformed. Past-tense. *All things are made new.*

The problem is we have bought into the idea that when we get born again we have to start fixing ourselves. Truth be told, you're perfect. Hebrews 10:14 (NIV) *For by one sacrifice he has made perfect forever those who are being made holy.* The quest isn't to restore the old you like you were some old beaten car. Instead we have to realize we are already new, a new car. The quest then is to truly discover all of the new car, and at the same time, stop driving the old car. **This is the transformation process**. The new you doesn't need to be restored, instead, it needs to be revealed. Revealing it happens through the process of growing in the word of God, seeing Christ's glory. Why? It is because we are to be conformed to the image of Christ. And Christ is in us, the hope of glory. There is much to say later about all of this, but I want to be certain you are introduced from the beginning that you are already new. So our becoming happens through the revelation of Christ.

Every one of us is becoming something. Take an eight year old for instance. Ask him what he wants to be when he grows up. We love to ask this question. Why? It is because we can see the potential on the inside of them. The same goes for a teenager. They have their whole lives ahead of them. They're becoming something; they're becoming someone. The reality is, no matter your age, you are becoming something. Every age that you are, you are *becoming*. When you wake up tomorrow, you are becoming. You are becoming either better or worse. You are becoming. Make no mistake. And, God has information and wisdom to help you become who He designed you to be.

Now, the world will offer you information on how to become something that you're not. That's the wrong information. God says, "*Don't be conformed to the pattern of the world but be transformed by the renewing of your mind.*" The *becoming* happens in the language that the mind processes. The mind communicates in a language. It communicates in knowledge. God teaches that to transform the mind we need new knowledge. You may ask, "*The knowledge of what?*" The mind needs the knowledge *of the likeness and image of His Son, Jesus*. What if we currently have the wrong knowledge of the image of Christ?

We would then have the wrong image of *ourselves*. Everyone has a different image and a different knowledge of who Christ is. This wrong image is created by the different things we hear, input from different sources, and the world's perception of Christ. Add all these up and it has created an image of who Christ is to you. That image may need some tweaking. Or it may be altogether wrong.

When I was in 5th grade, I would go to Sunday school class and they would portray an image of Christ. I remember the image was Jesus holding a baby lamb. You yourself may even recall seeing this same picture at some point in your life. That is the image I had of Jesus. Whenever I thought of Jesus, that image would pop into my mind. This was the Jesus I knew. He was very meek, very gentle, and very compassionate. I liked this Jesus. He is awesome. And, He was Mr. Turn-the-other-cheek. You could hit this guy as hard as you wanted and he would just turn the other cheek and say,

"Hit me again, whatever, I don't care!" He was very nice and he played with kittens and lambs all day long. THIS was the image I had of Jesus.

Now, when I was a young teen and I was coming of age, I wanted to emulate or start to become somebody I looked up to. Somebody I could connect to and somebody I could resonate with. I loved Clint Eastwood. Oh, come on! That's a man! Do you know what I'm talking about when I say, "That's a man!"? He's a man's man. He wasn't afraid of anything! He smoked, which was awesome. He was kind of wrinkly, always dirty, and you could almost smell him through the TV. He was a man. He wasn't scared of anything. He could walk into a room where ten people wanted to kill him and he would beat them all. The girls always loved him. As a young man I decided, "I want to be him." He's pure, unadulterated awesomeness, right? You remember, "I know what you're thinking, punk. Did he fire six shots or only five?"

Do you remember that? It was just awesomeness. He was an iconic, bigger-than-life man. I was becoming a man and I desired to be just like him. So, I have to smoke and talk quieter. The quiet talk was really cool, right? Clint Eastwood never yelled. If he was mad, he was just quiet. My dad had this same demeanour. My dad was the quiet-angry talk guy. If he was quiet talking to you, you were scared. My dad was kind of like Clint Eastwood. He never yelled at my brother or me. It was much worse. My dad would never shout, "Hey! I said to come over here and stop that!" He didn't do that. He would speak, in a quiet angry voice, "Come here." He would get right up close to you, "Don't you ever talk to your mother that way again." "Yes sir. I will never talk to my mom that way again!"

As a result, I was presented with a dilemma. I resonated with the manly icons and not with the image I had of Jesus. I was supposed to be a follower of Christ and I was supposed to become

Christ-like. Yet, I was not resonating with the blonde haired, blue eyed Jesus. (Which obviously, the painter of that Jesus did not study the Hebrew genetics.) My dilemma: Was I to become the turn-the- other-cheek compassionate person, or the Clint Eastwood and John Wayne man's man?

A man on a whole other level of manliness was Chuck Norris. Come on! I mean, there's nobody like him. Not only did he act in fighting scenes, but he was a world champion kick-boxer. He actually could fight. Chuck Norris is so, so tough, isn't he? When you think of Chuck Norris, you think of nails. I remember the movie Lone Wolf McQuade. Now don't be mad if I remember it wrong, I haven't watched it in years, but here is how I remember it. The movie was about a bunch of bad guys and the one lonely quiet guy. It was tough to make him angry, but once you did, then watch out. The bad guys took everything from him, and then one day...they killed his dog. That is what pushed him over the edge. Now he was really angry. I remember even as a kid laughing about that, like, that's the one that triggered you? The dog? Really? You watch him snap. He puts grease on his face and he goes to war with an entire village of bad guys, and he kills them all. I love this Chuck Norris. I heard he recently had a birthday, and at his birthday party he was handling cobras. He was just showing off because he's a tough guy. A cobra bit him, and here's the crazy thing, after five days of excruciating pain... the cobra finally died. That's because you don't bite Chuck Norris, you know what I'm saying? When he swims in the ocean, the sharks get in a cage. That's Chuck Norris. He's never had a near death experience, but death complains of having had a near Chuck experience. A lot of people didn't know that. He's that tough. He can kill two stones with one bird. He didn't even have to blow out his candles, out of fear the candles extinguished themselves. Chuck Norris, an iconic man.

The world gave me an image and definition of a man, and Sunday School gave me another image. I really didn't know what to do with it. As I got older, I started reading the Bible and I fell in love with the Scripture. As a 15 year old, I read about a Jesus that nobody had ever talked about in Sunday School. A new image of Jesus was beginning to reprogram my mind. He was the image of a powerful and radical man. He came on to the world stage at about the age of 30, and He didn't talk like anyone else, He didn't have the same message, He didn't conform, and He wasn't worried about whether people liked Him. He said what was on His mind, He hung around the wrong people, and He went against everything you could think of. I would read stories where He would call people snakes and a brood of vipers. He would get in people's faces. Pharisees and teachers of the law would come at Him and He would come right back. I thought to myself, "He's not turning the other cheek, and He's not Mr. Meek." I had to reconcile thoughts in my own mind. When He said, "Turn the other cheek," He must have meant something different from what I understood. When He said to be "meek," I always pictured him a mousy, wimpy guy. He wasn't that. What I came to realize was that my definition of meek had to be changed.

You and I know Jesus was exactly who He said He was. Maybe I had defined meek wrong? Maybe I defined turning the other cheek wrong? As I now read the Scripture, I saw a man who stood up. He said to a group of Pharisees and teachers of the law (my paraphrasing), "You know, my Father is God but do you know who your father is? Your father is Satan." Jesus said this to them in the temple, in front of everyone! He's like, "Yeah, Satan's your dad." Can you imagine doing this? He said to them, "Satan is a murderer and a liar and that's what you do. You want to kill me, but guess what? You're a liar and he's the father of all lies. When he lies, he speaks his native language, and that's your dad." Wow! Right? He was a tough guy. He could walk on water. Jesus went to battle with sickness. He went to battle with death, hell, and sin. He overcame. He was a warrior. As a result, I began to create a new image of Christ and the Word started to paint a different image on the inside of me. If we have the incorrect image of *Christ,* then we will have the incorrect image of *ourselves*.

As a young man, I found Jesus described in the book of Revelations. Look at the detail of His physical description in this passage:

Revelation 19:11-17 (NIV) *I saw heaven standing open and there before me was a white horse, whose rider is called Faithful and True. With justice he judges and wages war. His eyes are like blazing fire, and on his head are many crowns. He has a name written on him that no one knows but he himself. He is dressed in a robe dipped in blood, and his name is the Word of God. The armies of heaven were following him, riding on white horses and dressed in fine linen, white and clean. Coming out of his mouth is a sharp sword with which to strike down the nations. "He will rule them with an iron scepter." He treads the winepress of the fury of the wrath of God Almighty. On his robe and on his thigh he has this name written:* KING OF KINGS AND LORD OF LORDS.

Recapping the Scripture: *"I saw heaven standing open and there before me was a white horse, whose rider is called Faithful and True. With justice he judges and wages war. His eyes are like blazing fire, and on his head are many crowns."* See, He's like Clint Eastwood here. I wanted this from my Jesus, and I found it in the Bible! Continuing, *"His eyes are like blazing fire, and on his head are many crowns*." He's a leader of leaders, right? *He has a name written on Him that no one knows but He himself.* He's deep and mysterious. *He is dressed in a robe dipped in blood, and His Name is the Word of God. The armies of heaven were following Him, riding on white horses.* So, we get this picture that He wasn't just laying back in battle, but when it came to battle, He was leading the charge, correct? A massive army is lined up behind Him, because He's a leader of leaders. If there is a woman wanting a prince, this is the prince! But, He's not just any prince; He's the Prince of Peace. He's the King of Kings and Lord of Lords, coming out on His white horse to save the world. Come on, this Man is awesome!

Coming out of His mouth is a sharp sword with which to strike down the nations. He didn't just have a sword at His side; He had a sword coming out of His mouth. That's not easy to do, to hold a sword in your mouth. I applaud that, well done, Jesus!

On His robe and on His thigh He has this name written (And, may I point out, I think He was tattooed. I'm just saying, that writing on your skin is like a tattoo. If anyone is allowed to have a tattoo, its

Jesus, you know what I'm saying?) *"King of Kings and Lord of Lords."*

You know, if my thoughts of Jesus are of this poor, wretched, wimpy, struggling from town to town, persecuted, beaten up, and rejected man, I would have the wrong image of the overcomer that Jesus really was. I remember a preacher back in the early 90's preaching a message that said, "Jesus wasn't poor." He taught that Jesus did not live in poverty. Everybody that heard this message was astounded. They were asking, "What? How can this be true?" People would argue, "Yes, He was! Jesus was poor!" The preacher began to bear out the Scriptures. He taught how Jesus was visited by these kings from the east and they presented treasures to Him. Remember that in the Word? It was probably a lot! It's not that Mary *had* to birth Jesus in a manger. She birthed Him in a manger because there was no room at the hotel, not because they didn't have the money. People gambled for Jesus' clothes! For crying out loud! Not because He was the King of Kings! The Romans didn't even know that at this time. The Romans were just like, "That's some nice duds, man." They cut His clothes up into pieces and gambled for the fine linens. Jesus dressed very nice.

The disciples came to Christ and said, "We can't feed all these people. We can't find any food." They came to him because they knew He had the means to fix the problem. The disciples knew that they themselves did not have enough money to feed 15,000 people, so they approached Jesus. He had plenty of money. What does this show us? He had enough money to feed roughly 15,000 people out of His treasury. This is a Bible story and this is scriptural. When this preacher started teaching Jesus wasn't poor, people said, "Whoa, hold on!! Yes, He was poor!" Fast forward 20 years later, those same people who were against the teaching have now changed their minds. A new Jesus has been painted on the inside of them, and their minds have been renewed. Jesus was not poor. (He became poor on the cross. He also became sin and sickness on the cross, but before He was on the cross, He was neither sinful nor sick.) Jesus did have money while He was on the planet. This message that has been preached over the last 20 years painted a different image of who Jesus was, but back then it was a revolutionary teaching.

You know who the pastor was that taught that message? It was my dad. He preached the message that Jesus wasn't poor. And the message that freaked many out, at first, has now painted the right image of Jesus on the inside of many. I look at the scripture and realize, yes, He did have money. A new image of Jesus had now been painted. With a newly painted image of Jesus, people who were designed by God to accumulate wealth from the world and bring it to the kingdom of God were now set free and released to do this. They had a new image of Who Christ was.

What's my point? Our image of Christ can limit us in or propel us toward who we are becoming. If we have a wrong image, it will send us in the wrong direction. A right image of who Christ really is, painted correctly, is necessary in church. If we, the body of Christ, have the wrong image of who Christ is, what He looks like and who He was, then the church and Christ become far *less* attractive to the world. If we paint the right image of who Christ really is, then the church and Christ become far *more* attractive to the world. We want the bride of Christ to be glorious. The bride of Christ, the Church, we want her to be smoking hot. We desire Christ to be crazy attractive to the world. If we have painted the wrong image, we would find the world saying, "I don't know if I want to become that."

Allow me to paint a right image for you! When I was a young man, you might not know this from looking at me now, but I was little. I was a little person. In school, I was the one in the picture at the end of the row, because they lined us up tallest to shortest. Yes, that was my big day of humiliation! Let's just confirm that you're the littlest guy in the entire grade. LOL! Let's put you at the end of this line. And, let me just say, as a little guy, you have to overcome your littleness. The ladies were not super excited about the smaller guy, so I had to become super smooth to try to attract the ladies. I was always trying to figure out, as all guys do when they are in grade school and high school, what would attract the ladies. I figured that ladies wanted the sensitive, compassionate, emotional guy, a guy who's not afraid to cry. That's what I heard the girls saying. Okay, I can be that guy; I can be Mr. Sensitive, emotional and compassionate. What I found out was that girls did not want this at all! The wrong image had been painted in me that needed to be renewed. I observed that girls hung with guys who were trouble in class, "The bad boys." I had to learn to become that. The bad boy. What is attractive about the bad boy? Well, they're tough, can protect, they're strong, and girls are attracted to strength. Yes, girls want a sensitive man, but they also want a guy who's going be a great father and husband, compassionate, gentle, a defender, and a strong man. I learned as a young man that I had to walk differently. I could be tough. As I strutted, I thought, "You want me to be tough? I can be tough, got to be the tough guy." Guys want to emulate strong men, and ladies are attracted to strong men.

What happens when we give the world just one picture of Jesus? Here's a little Lamb of God Jesus. The world thinks, "If I want to become a Christian, I have to become a wimp! I don't resonate with that guy." However, if we can paint the picture of Jesus, in all of His facets, the world and the lost will find more in common with Him. Yes, I like the Lamb of God Jesus, but I also like Lion of Judah Jesus.

The book of Ezekiel paints four pictures of Christ.

> Ezekiel 1:10-11a (NIV) *[10]Their faces looked like this: Each of the four had the face of a human being, and on the right side each had the face of a lion, and on the left the face of an ox; each also had the face of an eagle. [11]Such were their faces.*

The four faces of Christ are found in the four gospels. God shows us a lion, an eagle, an ox and a man. I love that there was this lion side of Him. He had a roar. He was the *tear it apart* JESUS. He was the *go after it JESUS*. He was that crazy cool Jesus that would turn over tables, make a whip and command the room! He was also as gentle as a dove and as wise as a serpent. There are so many facets of who Christ really is. If we have the wrong image of Christ, we will have the wrong image of who we are becoming.

There is a story of Jesus attending The Feast of Tabernacles in Jerusalem. He made his way into the temple. He liked to go to the house of God, and He liked to teach. As He went in, He was kind of sneaking because the teachers of the Law and the Pharisees were trying to kill him. Jesus was not liked, and He had just healed a guy on the Sabbath Day. This really upset the Pharisees. They figured Jesus would show up at the Feast of Tabernacles, so they were looking for Him. Instead of showing up with His family, Jesus arrives a little bit late. He sneaks in the back door, and He started teaching. The Pharisees don't know it's the guy they're looking for! Why? Well, they didn't have Facebook and Twitter. No tweets or posts happened that day. They didn't even know exactly what He looked like, but they're watching for Him. Jesus begins to share who He is. The

Pharisees then start questioning Him, "Who are you?"

I am paraphrasing now from John 7:14-17. When the feast was half over, Jesus went up to the temple courts and began to teach. Then the Jewish leaders were astonished and said, "How does this man know so much when he has never had formal instruction?" So Jesus replied, "My teaching is not from me, but from the one who sent me. If anyone wants to do God's will, he will know about my teaching, whether it is from God or whether I speak from my own authority." This is the radical Jesus we read in the Word. This is the radical guy who didn't fit into the social norms. He didn't "fit in" with the times. In order to be a teacher of the Law, there was a process that you went through as a Hebrew. Jesus didn't formally go through that process. When He comes out teaching the Pharisees were upset!

There's a message in this passage for us. Many times, people think they have no business sharing about Jesus because they haven't been formally trained. They feel they must go to seminary school in order to share the Gospel. Hear my heart, I'm pro Bible College. But don't disqualify an anointed man or woman of God because they didn't have that training. Jesus didn't have any formal training and some people rejected Him for that. They said to Jesus, "Well, you haven't had formal training so I'm not to going listen to you." Can you imagine that? They would reject the Messiah because He didn't have a piece of paper, a diploma? You know, people still do this in our society today. Despite Scriptures like this, they will reject anointed pastors.

John 7:37-39 (NET) *On the last day of the feast, the greatest day, Jesus stood up and shouted out, "If anyone is thirsty, let him come to me, and let the one who believes in me drink. Just as the scripture says, 'From within him will flow rivers of living water.'" (Now he said this about the Spirit, whom those who believed in him were going to receive, for the Spirit had not yet been given, because Jesus was not yet glorified.)*

Look at this, my lion Jesus stood up and *shouted*. Earlier in the passage the Jewish leaders were wondering if this was Jesus, the One they had been looking for. Jesus stands up and *shouts.* Picture a large room with small seating areas all over the place. People were sitting, and teachers were teaching them in groups. Jesus was standing where they received the offering. He *shouts, "If anyone is thirsty, let him come to me, and let the one who believes in me drink. Just as the scripture says, 'From within him will flow rivers of living water.'"* If anyone is thirsty... what? Can you imagine everyone in the room looking at each other and saying, "Who is shouting?" Can you imagine all the people doing their own thing and minding their own business? There may have been some people in the corner singing songs. And Jesus *shouts, "If anyone is thirsty, come over here. Come on you guys, you're missing out! Let them come to Me and drink. Let the one who believes in Me drink. Just like the scripture says, 'From within him will flow rivers of living water.'"*

> John 7:40-44 (NET) *When they heard these words, some of the crowd began to say, "This really is the Prophet!" Others said, "This is the Christ!" But still others said, "No, for the Christ doesn't come from Galilee, does he? Don't the scriptures say that the Christ is a descendant of David and comes from Bethlehem, the village where David lived?" So there was a division in the crowd because of Jesus. Some of them were wanting to seize him, but no one laid a hand on him.*

Consider what they said: "No, this is not the Messiah. Because the *Christ doesn't come from Galilee*, right? And this Jesus guy, He came from Galilee. I mean, don't the Scriptures say the *Christ is a descendent of David and comes from Bethlehem, the village where David lived?"*

Let's move to John 8 now, as Jesus begins to reveal to us more of who He is:

John 8:14-18 (NET) *Jesus answered, "Even if I testify about myself, my testimony is true, because I know where I came from and where I am going. But you people do not know where I came from or where I am going. You people judge by outward appearances; I do not judge anyone. But if I judge, my evaluation is accurate, because I am not alone when I judge, but I and the Father who sent me do so together. It is written in your law that the testimony of two men is true. I testify about myself and the Father who sent me testifies about me."*

Jesus is letting them know that they don't actually know Him. They were asking Him who He was. That's the right question. "Give us a witness," they said. "It can't be him cuz he ain't from Bethlehem." That is interesting because you and I both know He was born in Bethlehem, right? But they didn't know this and so they rejected Him. They rejected Him because they didn't know where He came from. They just *assumed* he came from Galilee. So, in their assumption, they were saying if He had come from Bethlehem, they would believe in Him. Jesus is saying, "You don't know where I came from and that's your problem. Don't judge by outward appearances." You would think that Jesus would just clear this confusion up and say, "It may look like I came from Galilee, but really I came from Bethlehem." But he doesn't. He never says, "Oh hold on, time out, you're right. Scripture does say that the Messiah comes from Bethlehem and I was born there. Yep, that's right Pharisees, I was born in Bethlehem, and I am from the house of David. And look here," as he pulls papers from his briefcase, "I have the papers to prove it!"

Jesus doesn't give that information. He talked to them about where He came from, pointing to the Father, but He never told them the one thing they wanted to hear - that He came from Bethlehem. What's my point? He wanted them to seek him. "If you want to know me, you better dig. Don't just assume cuz you heard me talk for a few seconds that you know me." What was He saying? He was saying, *"Dig!"* Search for knowledge of Who Jesus is. Do you want to find out who Jesus is? It's not exposed on the surface, it's not plain in its appearance and the Bible is a great big book. I'm here to tell you the Bible is a great big book of Jesus and if you want to find who He really is, you need to dig. You can't just listen to what the world says about Jesus, you gotta get in that book and dig. If we want to find Jesus, we gotta dig. Let's go digging.

If we are being conformed into the likeness of Christ, through our knowledge of Him, then make sure you tweak out your knowledge of Him to agree with what He says about Himself. Dig to find out who Jesus is. Let the Word of God and the Holy Spirit bring you revelation of Christ, and the more you see Christ revealed, the more you can become the authentic person that God created and destined you to be.

Chapter Two

I AM not My Soul

As we adjust our knowledge of Christ to how the Bible displays Him we will find out that our Jesus is a Spiritual Being. Spirit first. He became flesh, but He is a Spirit. In this chapter, we need to remove our flesh and our soul from our identity as we continue to reveal Christ in us.

Psalm 42:5 (NIV) *Why, my soul, are you downcast? Why so disturbed within me? Put your hope in God, for I will yet praise him, my Savior and my God.*

David was speaking to his soul when he said, "What's wrong with you? Why are you down?" David wrote this and God saw fit to put it into His Bible, His word, for us to talk about, to think about, and to meditate on. Maybe David was in a funk. Have you ever been in a funk? David was down in the moment. Down times come. Have you ever experienced a down time?

My Dad shared with me when I was really young, "Never make a big decision when you are emotional." He gave me wisdom rooted in God's Word. When you are emotional, the voice of your emotions can scream so loud they drown out God's voice. We can either listen to the voice of our emotions or we can listen to the voice of God. One leads to winning. One leads to defeat and problems.

Let's say, for instance, you are at your job. You're upset at your boss because he's piling on the work load, and your emotions are high. You say, "Oh, I just can't handle this person. I'm so mad, I can't take it anymore. I quit." What happens then? Your bills come in the following week, and you realize you probably shouldn't have quit. You probably should have started looking for a job while you kept your current occupation. Or, maybe you should have just settled yourself down and had grace for the situation. Unfortunately, you were emotional and you made a decision to quit in the heat of the moment. Maybe you should quit, but quiet your emotions and wait for time to pass before making a decision like that.

"Oh, my God, I can't stand him anymore. I don't even think I love him anymore. I just want a divorce!" But do you want a divorce? Is that really what God has for you? Could your emotions be getting loud in that moment and now you're saying stuff you don't mean? We can all relate to this on some level. In our emotions, we can make bad decisions. It is wise to take a step back and allow God to speak to us. This is exactly what David was doing.

"*My soul why are thou downcast? Why so disturbed within me?*" David was taking a moment to ask his soul what the problem was. According to the current philosophy in this world, we do whatever feels good. The world teaches us to "go" with our emotions. However, what we need to do is take a moment to ask our soul what the problem is. The philosophy of the world is, "If it feels right it must be right." Following that philosophy leads to mistakes and brokenness. We don't follow the world's philosophies. We don't listen to what Hollywood says about marriage. We follow a philosophy an strategy that actually works, which is the Word of God. The Bible's philosophy and strategy is different from the world's. It doesn't follow what you're *feeling*.

David said this, "*My soul, why are you downcast? Why so disturbed within me? Put your hope in God, for I will yet praise*

His name, my Savior, and my God." David here is singing to himself. He is singing a song as he is talking to himself. "Hey, soul. What's your problem?" We might talk to someone this way. You run into somebody that's down and you might say, "What's going on with you, are you okay?" David is doing this to *himself*. He's having a conversation with his soul as though he is not his soul. "What's your problem soul?" He asks.

First, we need to establish what God is revealing, that you are *not* a soul. You have a soul, but you are *not* your soul. You are a *spirit*. Made in God's likeness and image. You are a *spirit* that has a body and a soul. God is Spirit. Jesus is Spirit.

> I Corinthians 15:44b-45 (NASB) *...If there is a natural body, there is also a spiritual body. So also it is written, "The first MAN, Adam, BECAME A LIVING SOUL." The last Adam (Christ) became a life-giving spirit.*

Adam was a living soul. Jesus is a life-giving Spirit. When you were born again you became a living spirit. You became a new creation. You are not like Adam. *You* are Christ-like. You were made into the likeness and image of God and His son Jesus. This now makes you a spirit. You are a spirit that has a body and a soul. What does your soul do? Your soul thinks, it feels, and it makes choices. It is your mind, will and emotions. It can actually live your life without you. Your soul could say, "I thought about it, I felt like doing it, and so I decided to do it!" It's very easy to be soul-led. I don't desire you to be soul led. I desire you to be *Spirit* led.

What did David do? David talked to his soul, "Why are you downcast, oh my soul?" He spoke to it, recognizing that his soul was *not* himself. If you allow your soul to think whatever it wants to think, it will think about stuff you should not. Your soul will say to you, "Boy, I wonder what it would be like if I weren't married." That is not a good thought to have if you are married. You should simply say, "No," to that thought. Your soul speaks again, "I wonder what my ex-girlfriend or ex-boyfriend is doing right now?" Not a great thought to engage your mind in if you are married. Your mind will think about stuff it shouldn't, which will develop emotions you should not be feeling, and the two of them will make decisions on your behalf. David found a way to take authority over his soul. David would have known about authority. He led great armies. He had mighty men. He was a king and ruler. He was knowledgeable on authority, and he also recognized that not everyone is obedient. David understood what it meant to use his authority. He began to take authority over his life and over his soul.

God has given you dominion and authority over your life. We all desire to be the boss at the work place. We desire to be in charge of the household. This is exactly why I have kids. For my whole life everybody bossed me around and told me what to do. Now, I have kids and I tell them what to do. I say, "Clean my house while I watch TV!" I am completely kidding! We all desire to be in charge. David demonstrates how you can take control of your life and how you can have authority.

I am not my flesh. I am not my soul. But I can be in charge of my flesh and my soul. Maybe I can become the coach of my life. I've got this amazing team around me. I have a mind, a will and some emotions. Maybe I could begin to coach them.

David asks, "Why am I listening to what my soul tells me? How long shall I take counsel in my soul? " (Paraphrased from Psalm 13:2 NKJV) The counsel of my soul is not always the correct counsel. We, as believers, have a different counselor. Jesus has provided a counselor which is the Holy Spirit. The Holy Spirit is a counselor who will never be wrong in your life. Where your emotional voice might be wrong, and where your thought processes might be wrong, the counselor, the Holy Spirit, will never lead you astray.

Psalm 119:25 (KJV) *"For my soul cleaveth to the dust."*

Your soul likes the dirty stuff. The soul holds on to the dust. It wants to wallow. Your soul thrives in the atmosphere of, "I'm down right now. I'm sad, I'm depressed, and I just want to wallow in my depression for a little while." It's like eating candy. It loves wrong attitudes, anger, bad thinking, drugs, lust, selfishness, and all the other dirt. It cleaves to the dust. How long will we take counsel in a soul that wants to cleave to the dust?

What would you do if you had a grumpy kid, moping around your house, acting as if life is so bad? What would you do if they came into your family room, slumped down on the couch and turned on the TV? What would you do? What would you do with a mopey kid? Would you just wait and hope they snap out of it? No! You would talk to them. "Hey! What's your problem?" That's what David did. David spoke to his soul and in my paraphrasing, he said, "You're like a mopey kid." He took authority over it. He inquired why it was downcast.

My family and I visited Disneyland recently, and we saw kids at Disneyland crying. You're at Disneyland! That's like the second happiest place on the earth. (God's sanctuary is the happiest place.) What on earth could you be crying about? Parents save up enough money to take their children to a place full of rides, churros, and magical goodness. Angels are literally singing, "Glory to God in the Highest," at Disneyland...and children are crying and upset! We witnessed one young kid entering the gates of Disneyland pitching the hugest fit, screaming, "I don't even want to be here! This place stinks!" Whoa! They hadn't even walked through the front gates of the park yet. In the same way, our soul does this to us. Our soul will say, "I don't even want to be here." The soul gets mad about stuff. The soul wants you to be angry and he wants you to be sad.

You need to talk to your mopey soul. No person has the power to make you feel anything. Did you know that? We have a choice in the emotions that we have. If, for example, someone has upset you and you now feel angry, just know that they didn't make *you* angry. They made your *soul* angry. Nobody has the power to make you anything. People don't have the power to make you angry. You allowed yourself to get angry and offended. There's a difference.

Ask your soul, "What's your problem?" David asked. A power of reflection happens when we examine ourselves. David didn't ignore that he was feeling downcast. He didn't pretend like he wasn't mad. He examined his soul and took the time to ask why it was upset.

Sometimes Christians make the mistake of pretending like they're happy. I'm just going to pretend. I'm just going to bury my emotions. I'm sad right now, but I'm just going to bury it and put a smile on it and I'll shove it down deep in my heart. The more sadness I feel, I'll take it, and I'll bury it down, and I'll shove it deep down in my heart. And just when I think the emotions are going to explode, I'll smile on the outside and I'll push it down a little more, because I'm going to be happy. This strategy does not work.

David recognized he was dealing with a downcast soul. He was willing to make the admission to himself and all of us. He was saying, *"Something is wrong within myself."* Anything you bury in your heart will grow. Bury love and it will grow love. Bury sadness and it will grow depression. Bury lust and it will grow perversion. We have to examine ourselves just like David did. You have to take time to ask yourself, "Hey, what's wrong with you?" Many times we don't even know what's wrong with us. Have you ever done that? You were just mad. You don't even know why you're mad. That is when we need to self-reflect and ask ourselves, "Why are you mad? Why are you down, oh my soul?" This is a powerful question.

I remember growing up, how mad my brother would get if there was peanut butter in the jelly jar. My brother, being three-and-a-half years older than me, used to tease me to no end. He was bigger and older, but I wasn't helpless. I had to find ways to get back at him. He would get so mad if there was peanut butter in the jar of jelly. My brother hates peanut butter. Hates it! Every morning he would make himself a bowl of cereal and jelly toast. He loved his jelly. When I realized how mad peanut butter in his jelly jar made him, I plotted my revenge. I think it's important to realize your triggers in life. I knew my brothers trigger, it was peanut butter! Here's the thing, my mom would make peanut butter and jelly sandwiches for my school lunch. When she would make it, she would use the same knife for both the peanut butter and jelly. As a result, peanut butter would sometimes make it into the jelly jar. Oh, my brother would get so mad. But, ya know, you never get mad at mom. You don't ever yell at mom, because that's never going to work out for you. So, whenever he got upset with mom, I knew that something big was going to happen. I enjoyed this. He was finally getting in trouble. What I learned to do, when no one was around, I would take peanut butter and scoop it into the jelly. I'm not saying this was Christian behavior. I'm just telling you what I did.

We need to know our triggers in life. What triggers you? Maybe somebody got some peanut butter in your jelly, and now you are upset. What triggers you? Maybe on Facebook you saw that Ted took his wife Nancy to Fiji. You're looking at the phone and saying, "She gets to go to Fiji! My husband never takes me to Fiji. Why don't I get to go to Fiji?" In that moment, what was a nice Facebook post now has you all stirred up and jealous. Instead of being happy for Nancy, you are now mad at your husband. He hasn't done anything wrong, but you are mad at him. "You never take me to Fiji!!" What happened here? What triggers us?

What makes our soul downcast? David asked the question but he didn't wait for the answer. He said, "*Why, my soul, are you downcast? Why so disturbed within me? Put your hope in God...*" I love his reaction. David spoke to his soul, "Why are you downcast?" but he did not wait for a response. He asked his soul the question and then directed his soul what to do. He didn't allow his soul to have an excuse. An excuse will always keep you trapped in your unhappiness. Ted says, "Well, I'm just tired today. I didn't get a good night sleep and so I'm grumpy." There's the excuse. Now, you will be grumpy all day. You will make everybody in the house miserable. You will make everybody at your job miserable. All because you're grumpy and you didn't get enough sleep.

You need to ask your soul, "What is your problem?" The answer God has will always be the same. Put your hope in God.

"Pastor, I don't have enough money to meet my bills. I'm upset right now. I'm depressed." Now, you will be depressed. Your co-worker approaches you and says, "Hey, how are you doing today?" You reply, "Oh, I don't know. Things are not that great. My bills are out of control and I don't have enough money." You need to ask your soul, "What is your problem?" God's answer will always be the same. Put your hope in God.

David did not wait for his soul to answer. He instructed his soul what to do. *Put your hope in God.* He didn't even wait for an answer. He was saying, "I don't care what your answer is, soul. You just need to put your hope in God." You don't have enough money for the mortgage? Put your hope in God. Your marriage is in trouble? Put your hope in God. Your teenager is making wrong choices? Put your hope in God. It doesn't matter what your problem is or what your soul's excuse is, if you put your hope in God, your soul makes a turn around.

Hebrews 6:19 (NIV) *We have this **hope** as an **anchor** for the soul, firm and secure.*

Hope is an anchor for your soul. The soul is like a vessel in the ocean. A captain will lower the anchor when he needs the vessel to hold its position. In the same way you need to drop anchor. The soul will wander, it needs to be anchored. Put your hope in God. It will anchor your soul. Hope will stop the flip flopping between sadness, depression and anger. When you receive bad news, stay in hope. When it looks like a storm is coming, stay in hope. Always hope. Let hope become the prison you live in, immoveable and unshakeable. Anchored in hope, you will make better decisions.

> 1 Peter 1:13 (NIV) *Set our hope on the grace of God. Therefore, with minds that are alert and fully sober, set your hope on the grace to be brought to you when Jesus Christ is revealed at his coming.*

You need to set your hope on His grace. His grace reminds us of all that He gives us that we don't really deserve. You may feel like you don't deserve His blessing, but grace tells us that because of the works of Christ you must know that God is blessing you, that His hand is on your life, that He loves you exactly as you are, that He accepts you because of your faith in Jesus, that He sees you as righteous, and He sees you as holy. His angels are going before you and preparing victory on your behalf. You need to set your hope on the grace of God.

"Pastor, my sorrow runs deep. I'm a deep person. My wounds are way to the core. My struggle is deep and dark. You have no idea where I came from or what I came out of." David's soul was in that dark place and he spoke to it.

Psalm 42:7 (NIV*) "Deep calls to deep in the roar of your waterfalls; all your waves and breakers have swept over me."*

David was expressing that his wounds were deep, but God said, "I'm deeper. I'm far deeper than your wounds." You thought your wounds went to the core of who you are but when you received Jesus, the hope of God, and the love of God went even deeper than your wounds. There is a fountain and a well inside of you that is even deeper than your sorrow. The ocean of love God has for you is even deeper than the defeat you felt, even deeper than the wound that you've carried with you for 30 years. It's even deeper than your pain. What can happen is the voice of your pain and sorrow can try to speak to you. It will try to speak into your future. But even deeper within you, is God calling you. He calls to the deep parts of you and says, "You may feel sorrow, but I have victory, and praise, and gladness for you. You're broken but I have wholeness for you." God's deep is calling to your deep and it says, "He was beaten for your transgressions and He was bruised for your iniquities. And, by His stripes you have been healed." It doesn't matter how deep your pain is, the love of God is unfathomable. His mercy is never ending. His grace will never run out of depth for you in your life. His deep is calling to your deep. It doesn't matter how deep your despair may be. Remember, therefore, if anyone is in Christ, the new creation has come: The old has gone, the new is here!

2 Corinthians 5:17 (NKJV) *If anyone is in Christ, he is a new creation.*

If ANYONE is in Christ... Who? *Anyone.* This promise does not come with a prerequisite. It does not say that you have to be free of your addiction. It does not say that you have to be a loving person 100% of the time. It just simply says, "*If anyone is in Christ, he is a new creation. All things have passed away. Behold, all things have become new.*" This means your soul is brand new. The wounds of the past have been erased. You say, "Well, Pastor, I get angry fast. It's just part of my makeup. That's my genetics. We just have a temper in my family. That's how we've always been." No! Do not dig up the dead, crucified old man that doesn't exist anymore, but instead, replace it with your brand-new soul. Your brand new soul does not come with any garbage. God is not trying to fix the *old* you. He gave you a brand new you. He is not trying to restore the old clunker and the dents of who you used to be. He erased who you used to be and started a fresh, brand new you.

When I was a kid, I had one pair of shorts. They were hand-me-down, cut-off jean shorts from my brother. Back in the 80's when you cut off jeans to make shorts, you didn't cut them at the normal knee length like nowadays. You would cut them way up above the thigh. It was not a good thing. I would never post a picture of myself in them. In grade school, my mom cut those jeans so short that it went right through the pockets. That's how short these shorts were. When visiting a friend's house, my brother and I would like to bring toys to play with. Our favorite toys were matchbox cars. My brother would stuff his shorts with like 15 cars, but I could only take two. I didn't have pockets, so I had one for each hand. As a result, I had really short shorts...and envy. I would watch him play with all his cars. One day my parents bought me a brand new pair of shorts. My new shorts had pockets that worked. Can you guess how many times I still went somewhere with just the two cars? A lot! My mind was programmed to think that I had holes in my pockets, and I would forget to pack my new shorts with cars. How many of us live as though we still have holes in our pockets? We're living as though we still wear the old shorts. Look, God gave you some new shorts and they have pockets. Pack them full. Stop acting like you have holes in your shorts. Stop acting like the old you. You are brand new.

We recently got a dog in our family. He's a beautiful little Biewer Terrier. When we got him, the breeder told us he was the runt of the litter. He was the smallest dog and he was the last one to be adopted. We named him Captain Jack Sparrow. He's a great dog and he's super smart. When he eats, though, he will grab a whole mouthful of food, walk pretty far away, drop the food, and then eat it. Then, he will walk back to the bowl and repeat the same behavior. He does this every time he eats his food. My daughter, Katy, was observing this and asked, "Why is he doing that?" I said, "Because, when you're the runt, you learn to grab your food and get away from your brothers and sisters so they won't take it out of your mouth." This was a survival mechanism he learned. He learned that in order to survive, he had to grab what he could, as quick as he could, and make a fast get-away. Jack lives in *our* family now. He's in a safe environment. He's away from the old environment, but he still acts as though he has to guard his food. I will say to Captain Jack, "Look, you're safe, puppy. You're in a brand- new house, with a brand-new family. Nobody is going to take the food out of your mouth. You are healed. You're set free. Why are you still wearing your prison clothes? Why are you still acting like you're in prison, when you've been set free? Just stand there and eat!" You know what it took? We repositioned some furniture in our family room, which caused the spot where Jack would hide and eat to be taken. When he lost the space where he would go to eat, he began to eat at his bowl. In the same way, God moves His promises into the spaces where we hide, where we kept our past, where we built our walls. God moves in with all of His promises. He replaces the space where our addiction used to hide. When you replace your brokenness with God's promises, you'll be set free from the old ways of thinking.

Sometimes we just need a reminder, to remember that we are a new creation.

David did this. He began to remember.

> Psalm 42:6a(NIV) *My soul is downcast within me; therefore, I will remember you.*

Maybe, we need to take a moment with our soul and remind ourselves of good things. Maybe, in your marriage, you need to go back and remember your wedding day. Remember how you felt. Remember the time your husband held your hand and you were so in love. Remember the time when your wife did something extra in your life. Can you go back and remember the day you first met? How about remembering when you first got that job you prayed for? How did it feel when you were hired and God answered your prayer? How about remembering those times when you couldn't make rent, but somehow God was faithful and provided? Let's take a moment to remember the good things in our life.

I tell my son, when he is down and pouty, the fastest way back to happiness is through the conduit of gratefulness. When our soul is downcast we need to get back into some thankfulness. Can we learn to be thankful?

Psalm 42:6 (NIV) *"My soul is downcast within me; therefore, I will remember you, **from the land of the Jordan, the heights of Hermon—from Mount Mizar."*** (Bold added for emphasis.)

When David spoke about the *land of Jordan* he was referring to a low place.

Jordan was a lower region. He was showing us that he will remember God in the low places of his life. On the contrary, when he mentions the *heights of Hermon*, he was referring to remembering God in the peaks of life. Hermon is the highest mountain in all of Israel. It is 7,334 feet above sea level. And, Hermon means sanctuary. David was saying to God, "I will remember you at the highest points of my life, when I was in your sanctuary and I felt your love come upon me, when I felt chains break off me and I felt the emotion of God come on me. I felt your great hug."

How many have felt that moment with God? You were praising God's name in the sanctuary for His victories in your life, and you experienced a moment with God. David was praising God in the highlight of his life and remembering those times when God was faithful in the sanctuary.

Then David says, *"And, I will remember you at **Mount Mizar**." **Mizar*** means "small." What was David saying? I will remember God in the small things. I will remember You on the way down. You know, David had low moments in his life. When he was close to becoming king and was chased down by Saul, this was a low moment. Saul wanted to kill David. David had to run for his life for many years. He was on the way down, but he never stopped remembering God's goodness. And, when he was on his way back up to the very top and made King, he remembered God. David learned to remember God in the small things and the big things in life, in the low places and in the high places.

My soul, what's your problem? Maybe you need to remember the great things in your life. Remembering what God has done can pull you out of having a downcast soul.

Psalm 42:4 (NIV) *These things I remember as I pour out my soul: how I used to go to the house of God under the protection of the Mighty One with shouts of joy and praise among the festive throng.*

He talks about remembering before he asks his soul what is wrong. Then he talks about remembering after he questions his soul. He made a "remember sandwich" out of his downcast soul. "*How I used to go to the house of God under the protection of the Mighty One with shouts of joy and praise among the festive throng.*" What was he saying? How about you? Do you remember when you used to get excited about going to church? Remember the excitement of going to the sanctuary to praise God and hear His Word? No amount of rain or lack of sleep could keep you out of God's house on a weekend. There was no football game more important. David is revealing himself in this moment. He was being honest with himself. He said, "Remember, when you used to be excited about running to God's house?" David was compelled to lead the people to

God's house. This *is* the great commission! Go out into all the world and make disciples. Jesus said, "Go out and compel them to come into my house, that my house might be full." David was compelling a *festive throng* to God's house. The greatest fulfillment comes in our lives when we lead people into God's house. It does not matter how down and out you could be, when you lead someone to God's house you feel fulfilled. It is what Christ has called us *all* to do! Want joy and fulfillment? Lead someone to church. Do you remember when you were so excited about God's house and Christianity that you couldn't keep your mouth shut? If church is the equipping center for the saints, then it is Jesus' chief discipleship center.

David is calling his soul to remember God. Our soul sometimes forgets God. In Deuteronomy the Lord tells the Israelites that they will forget Him when they come into the Promised Land. Do we forget God after He restores us? Have we forgotten to bring others to the high place where God placed us? Do we get to such a place of fruitfulness and prosperity that we forget to invite people to God's house? We must be careful not to forget the joy of leading people to the house of God. I believe God has called the local church to influence the city and state you live in!

Defeat and trials happen in our lives. God never said that you would not face trials and circumstances in your life. They come, but we can snap out of the emotions that come too; we don't have to be led by our soul. We don't have to carry yesterday's wounds into our tomorrow. Let's speak to our souls today! God has been faithful and He is a good God. I wave goodbye to the day of defeat and sadness. I choose to put my hope in God. I am going to remember the times that God was victorious in my life. My soul will find rest with God, because He has given me the victory. Can you say that to your soul as well? Maybe you feel a little beat up and defeated. It is halftime and your soul could use a pep talk. "Hey soul, remember God's goodness in the low times and the high times, in the small things and the big things. Remember God, and put your hope in Him, for I will yet praise His Name."

Chapter 3
Overcoming our Strength Famine

You are not your soul or your body. You are a spirit. Knowing who and where you come from helps determine who you are. If you want to know more about a historical figure, you begin to look into where they were born, where they grew up, and what their family is like. In the same way, a Christian comes from Christ.

You are in Christ and He is in you. So the merge happens by revealing more of Him.

If I am being conformed to Christ by revealing who He is, then the traits revealed to me in the Word will come to life in my personal story as they are discovered. An important note about the weaknesses often found in us: we don't overcome weakness by becoming stronger through some process. Instead we become stronger by revealing the strength of Christ. You cannot make Christ stronger than He is, and He is in you, just waiting for you to let that strength manifest in your weakness.

In this chapter, I want to increase your strength by revealing the strength of Christ. I personally cannot increase your strength. I don't have the capability or the capacity to affect your strength. What I do have is the Word of God. The Word of God contains the capacity and the power to create change inside of you. A pastor cannot change people. I can't do that.

However, the Word of God, the Seed of God is incorruptible and it has the capacity to bring change. It has the power to reveal the transformation that God has already made to our lives.

Christianity around the world, for the most part, has painted a wrong image of Christ. Not necessarily wrong in the sense that it's incorrect information, but wrong in the sense that it's missing many facets of who Christ is. The part that we tend to leave out in Christianity, as a whole, is the strong part of Christ, the Lion of Judah. We have done a great job talking about the meekness of Christ, the Lamb of God, the turn-the-other-cheek Jesus. But I don't think that the world, as a whole, or Christianity as a whole, has done a good job of painting the powerful side of Christ. The warrior and the mighty victorious side of Christ has not been clearly displayed. This has caused Christians and churches to operate out of weakness. There has been a strength famine in us, in church, and it needs to be remedied.

Joel 3:9-10 (NET) *Prepare for a holy war! Call out the warriors! Let all these fighting men approach and attack! Beat your plowshares into swords, and your pruning hooks into spears! Let the weak say, 'I too am a warrior!'*

Sounds like a battle. God also asks us to prepare to enter into His rest. But we are in a fight, and He gives us the armor of the Lord and a sword of the Spirit for the battle. (Paraphrased) "Take your farming tools and make them into weapons, we have some territory to take!"

Sometimes the reason we are met with defeat or we're tempted to quit is because of a lack of strength. We were so busy turning the other cheek with everything around us; we forgot that Jesus didn't put up with darkness at all. Sometimes we are missing out on the victory, because we didn't bring the *fight*. Sometimes the devil delivers a package to your house. He delivers a sickness, or he delivers some junk you don't deserve, and you accept it. I find Christians signing for it and saying, "Oh, I'll just live with this for the rest of my life." Maybe your child has been diagnosed with this thing, so now here are some pills he needs to take. Christians will say with their best defeated voice, "Well, okay," and they sign the delivery receipt. They accept it. They essentially sign on the dotted line. They forgot (or maybe didn't know) to beat their plowshares into a sword, to draw up a battle line, and say, "NO!"

Other times Christians give up too fast. They said, "NO," for a week and then they gave up. Or they said, "NO," for two weeks, didn't see a result, and decided to give in. Listen, it's a war, and we have to fight the good fight of faith.

My wife Kelli and I said, "NO," to my daughter's diagnosis of asthma. When she was born the physician diagnosed a life-time of asthma. We said, "NO," to it for five years. For five years she was on stimulants and breathing machines in the mornings and evenings. We talked about this the other day with our daughter, Katy. She remembers, as a little girl, sitting on our bed in the mornings, with her breathing machine while we watched TV. She just thought that was a normal way of life, but my wife and I never accepted it as normal! Five years of fighting later, she came out of asthma. Fast forward ten years from that, she ran cross country in high school. That's a miracle! We have to reveal that our Jesus is a lion, He is a mighty warrior, a fighter ready to go mano-a-mano with whatever satan brings. In fact, He already fought and won. He is our fighting Jesus.

I went to my son Logan's basketball game. Now, Logan has an older brother, Matthew, so he is not foreign to conflict in our family. He's used to battling with a kid who's twice his size. When it comes to fighting and being a little boy, he's good, he's strong, he's ready. When another kid tries to take the ball from Logan, he's like, "Oh no you don't! Get out of here!" My son Christian, on the other hand, was a whole different ball player. Christian is our eldest. After him came his sister, Katy. Christian and Katy rarely had conflict — besides normal brother and sister arguments. No fist fights or wrestling happened between them. Christian was not an aggressive basketball player. He started playing basketball when he was 8 or 9 years old and I remember his first game. He was bouncing the ball and a little kid came up and knocked it out of his hands. You could just see his little heart break. It was as if he was saying, "Oh, how could you? I would never do that to you." He looked at me, "Daddy, did you see that? He stole the ball from me!" He looked so violated. And this is how many Christians are responding to the attacks in our world. We act like victims, we don't respond with strength. The enemy steals from us, he takes our stuff and we just go, "How could you do such a thing to me?"

My wife's reaction to the ball being stolen from Christian was like, "What is wrong with our son? Why doesn't he go get the ball back?" She'd yell, "Go get him!" I don't know if she said this, but what I heard was, "Go punch him! Knock that little boy out!" After the game, I took Christian aside and explained to him, "When the ball is taken from you, don't let that happen; take it back." I began to tell him what to do when conflict arises. You know, the next game he did it again, the behavior didn't change. See, I was trying to tell him *what to do* instead of telling him *who he was.* When I changed my philosophy, I got a completely different result. Using a godly principal, I went to him and said, "Here is what your dad (myself) would do if I were playing basketball, and somebody took the ball from me." I began to run him through a routine. "Come towards me Christian, and try to take the ball from me." I'm holding the ball and I'm like, "Come get it out of my hands." Then I swiped it away fast, and I got those elbows going. "That's what I would do," I explained to him. I started banging into him with my body, backing him up, and being aggressive.

What was I doing? I was sharing with him what I would do. Once he learned what his *dad* would do, he thought, that's who I come from. If that's what my daddy would do, then that's what I'll do. When the strength of Christ is revealed, it will automatically make you stronger. This is how God changes us. How does God handle satan? How did Jesus descend into the depths of the earth? Who was it that said He'd be the strength within us, and how strong is He?

What's my point? Our behavior changes when we find out who we are. We find out who we are when we see more of Jesus revealed. Who you are is who you came from. You didn't come from the place you were born. You came out of the Living God. When you look at the transformation process, you may think if you change your behavior, it will change who you are. We all think we've got to change our behavior. Ever heard of New Year's resolutions? I've got to change my behavior and that will make me a better person. We focus on changing our behavior, but it doesn't work. We change our behavior for a week or two and we're back to the same old thing again. It didn't work. Why doesn't it work? It doesn't work because it's based on an old philosophy. The old philosophy is the Law, the Old Covenant, which says, "Here, do this and that'll make you a better person." The Law didn't work. What I mean is God gave the Law to the Israelites on Mount Sinai to make them a better and more blessed people. If they could do the rules, God would bless them. If they didn't, well, it was a curse. The Law makes sense to our reasonable mind, but it failed miserably. The reason it failed was because God wanted to show us that it would not work. He proved it to us generation after generation. Even in the beginning, God said to Adam, "Don't eat the fruit and life will be golden." What happened? You see, we still think the rules will help us change our behavior and that will make us a stronger person. We think we can change our behavior and *that* will change who we are. We've got it backwards. Realize *who* you are and that will change your behavior!

I've heard it preached many times; repentance will lead us to God's goodness. It's a message that makes reasonable sense. But that is not what God said. The Book of Romans 2:4b (NKJV) says, *"The goodness of God leads you to repentance."*

Y'all got it backwards. What's on the inside of you will determine what you do over time. God changes where you came from, because who you are is based on where you came from. Where did you come from you may ask? I was born in Janesville, Wisconsin. Bull! I was still dead when I was born in Janesville, Wisconsin. I did not come to life until I became born of God. I am born of God! Where did you come from? YOU are born of God! Where did I come from? I am born of God. All of the tragedy, abuse, and crisis you faced in your formative years no longer have the power to impact you. The world and its mess tried to form you into who you are, but when you received Jesus you were transformed. The past happened to the old you, not the new you. You were born again.

> 1 Peter 1:23 (NKJV) *Having been born again, not of corruptible seed but incorruptible, through the word of God which lives and abides forever.*

You are born of an incorruptible seed. How do you corrupt something that's incorruptible? You are no longer capable of being corrupt, because you are born of an incorruptible seed. You can't even corrupt yourself. We walk around trying to be good Christians, trying to change, instead of focusing on *who we are*. If I can just focus on who I am, my behavior will change! If I think I'm an addict, I'll continue to be addicted, even though I abstain. Even though I abstain, I'm living in a personal hell, because I want the addiction, because I'm an addict. God says, "No, when you become born again you become a new creation." We have got to settle this. Let's settle this once and for all. I get it, the world tells you you're still an addict, but they don't know what they're talking about. When you were born again, you became a new creation. Old things passed away. God wiped away your past. Now you're brand new.

We sold our house recently and built a new house. Now we are in our new house and it's wonderful. Imagine if I said to my wife, "I have a big week this week. I gotta fix the roof." She would say, "Fix the roof? What are you talking about? It's a brand new roof." What if I replied, "Oh, not this house, I meant I'm working on the old house. I have to go fix that roof." She'd be like, "It's not even our house, why would you go back and fix the old house?" This is how people live their Christianity. You have a new house, so why are you trying to fix the old house?

You pay $150 an hour to a psychologist to tell you who's to blame for why you are the way that you are. They get to the part in the therapy session when you find out who is to blame for your behavior. It's your daddy's fault or whoever, and you're like, "Oh good, now I can blame that person." But guess what? You're still the same. You didn't change. Give me the $150 an hour, please. Just send me the money. I'll take your $150 if you want to throw it away! That therapist is just going to give you some pills anyway! But God does it differently. You are not that person anymore. Your daddy is God now. You received a new pedigree. You are a brand-new creation born of incorruptible seed. People dig up their old man, but, he's dead. What do you do with dead people? You put them in a coffin and bury them. What do we do? People say, "I need to transform myself, so let's go dig up the body." We dig up the body and we say, "You know what's wrong with you?" Then we try and fix it. It's dead! Just let the body decay. You are not even that person anymore. You are not an addict, you are not weak, you are not all the junk that everybody puts on you, you are none of those things. You are the incorruptible seed of the living God.

I was crucified in Christ, nevertheless I live, yet not I, but Christ that lives in me. Who lives in you? Christ. Stop focusing on changing the behavior and focus on Who Christ is.

Hebrews 12:2 (NIV) *fixing our eyes on Jesus, the author and perfecter of our faith who for the joy set before him endured the cross, scorning its shame, and sat down at the right hand of the throne of God.*

Just look at Jesus. You want to make a change to your life? Well then, here's Jesus. Here's what you look like. As He's revealed in me, I find I have access to the same strength that's within Him, because He's in me. That is what I'm born of. Don't focus on changing your behavior. *Focus on Christ and the behavior will change.* The addiction just falls off when you recognize that you're not an addict. The anger just falls off when you realize this is not you anymore.

A man named Frank Willis, a security guard, was working his shift late one night. He worked in Washington, D.C.. As he was making his rounds, he noticed that the doors to one of the interior offices had tape on it. Someone had taped the metal plate that pops out so that the door opens and closes easily and doesn't lock behind itself. He thought, "That's strange!" So, he ripped the tape off. He wasn't alarmed by it. He just thought one of the employees probably did it sometime during the day. Twenty minutes later he decided to check that door again. When he went back to the door it was taped again. He acted as if he didn't notice, went to his office, and called the police. The police arrived and found four burglars hidden in that building. That building was called Watergate. That scenario, as it was investigated, eventually led to the resignation of a United States President, Richard Nixon. One piece of tape changed the future of an entire nation. *In the same way, one revelation of Christ can impact your future.* Just one little revelation can totally turn your life around. You've been a victim of your circumstance, but suddenly, this revelation of the strength of Christ can turn you around. We start to see the Lion of Judah, Christ our fighter and our warrior. You don't have to change yourself, you just reveal Who Christ is and you receive it.

When we think of strong Bible heroes, we have to consider Samson. There is a story in Judges 15 I'd like to tell. A thousand blood-thirsty Philistines had come to the Israelites looking for Samson. They wanted Samson dead. The Philistines said to the Israelites, "Give us

Samson!" The Israelites outnumbered the Philistines three-to-one, but they were still afraid. They were operating out of weakness. Sometimes we operate out of weakness, because we've forgotten who is on the inside of us. The Israelites went to Samson and said, "We have to hand you over to the Philistines!" Samson was like, "Awesome! Tie me up. Let's see what happens." Samson sees this as an opportunity to get among the Philistines and really have a good fight. He is basically like a Trojan horse as the Israelites bind him and deliver him to the Philistine army. Upon delivery, the Philistines came rushing at our hero, but Samson breaks free, grabs a donkey jawbone and slaughters all 1,000 of the Philistines. Now, I've seen some movies where Chuck Norris takes on about twenty bad guys. Imagine if it were 1,000. We would find that scene unbelievable. That is exactly what happened when the Spirit of the Lord came upon Samson. Samson did the unbelievable. Likewise, when the Spirit came upon Jesus, Jesus did the unbelievable! Jesus said that greater works would we do. Samson is a picture of our Jesus. In this way, Samson reveals to us the strength of Christ. He's a tough guy. (He's just like Jesus, and Jesus ain't scared.)

Here we get a picture of the crucifixion in this story. Why? Samson's own people gave him over to the enemy for death. This is the picture of crucifixion. This was also the plan Jesus had. Take me to the enemy and let me show you what I can do! Jesus wanted to reveal His strength to us. What was He showing us? I'm a fighter, I'm a warrior, and I can kick some tail with a donkey jawbone. I can destroy the power of darkness and the enemy that comes at you, because I am in you and I will fight for you.

Now, here's the weird part, the donkey is *you*. I know, that's bad, right? But look, we are similar to donkeys. We have a free will, we are kind of rebellious, and we don't like people telling us what to do!

Exodus 13:13 (ESV) *Every firstborn of a donkey you shall redeem with a lamb, or if you will not redeem it you shall break its neck. Every firstborn of man among your sons you shall redeem.*

In the same scripture, first born of a donkey or a man, is God's. The donkey is you and me. The donkey is us. Point your finger to yourself and say, "I'm a donkey!"

What was God saying about the donkey jawbone? He was saying, "I'll fight for you but I need your mouth. You will be *My* mouthpiece. I'll fight for you, but you have to stop saying the wrong thing. You have to start saying what I'm saying." God will destroy 1,000 of them and He is your strength! You don't have to be strong. He is your strength. Just give Him access to your mouth and He'll blow it up. Praise God! He's a fighter and He's an overcomer. He is your lion, *The Lion of*

Judah. There is a time to turn your cheek, because you don't need to have a battle every time. There's a time for meekness but it's not all the time. There's a time for strength and there's a time for war.

We have to reveal Who Christ is and that will change us. When we see Samson as a picture of Christ's strength, we unlock the strength that He has already planted in us. You aren't changing your behavior, instead, you are revealing who Christ is, and your behavior changes automatically. As you reveal who Jesus is, when He says, *"let the weak say **I am** strong,"* the *"I am"* you're pulling on is *Christ*. He's the GREAT I Am. You are going to access the strength of the Lord. In the Bible, there is revelation after revelation of Who Christ is. It is not just in Matthew, Mark, Luke and John. It's in every book of the Bible. You can find Christ revealed in every book.

In Genesis, He was the seed of the woman. In Exodus, He was the great I Am.

In Leviticus, He was the sacrificial lamb. In Numbers, He was the water and the rock. In Deuteronomy, He was the daily manna. In Joshua, He was the God of my salvation. In Judges, He's the judge of all the nations. In Ruth, He's the kinsman redeemer. In 1 and 2 Samuel, He's the anointed king. In Kings and Chronicles, He's the reigning king. In Ezra, He's my builder. In Nehemiah, He is my restorer. In Esther, He's my mediator. In Job, He is my ransom. In Psalms, He's the king of all kingdoms. In Proverbs, He's the giver of all wisdom. In Ecclesiastes, He's the creator of all seasons. In Song of Solomon, He's the husband to His church. In Isaiah, He's God with us. In Jeremiah, He's the righteous branches. In Lamentations, He is the weeping prophet. In Ezekiel, He's the man with four faces, but in Daniel, He was the fourth man in the blazes. In Hosea, He's my faithful provider. In Joel, He's the baptizer of fire. In Amos, He's my burden bearer. In Obadiah, He's my mighty Savior. In Jonah, He rescued me from the pit. In Micah, He's the messenger with beautiful feet. In Nahum, He's my avenger. In Habakkuk, He's the resurrected, anointed one. In Zephaniah, He's the taker of my punishment. In Haggai, He's the glory that surpassed the former glory. In Zechariah, He's the enthroned priest and the builder of His church. In Malachi, He's the refiner. In Matthew, He's the Messiah. In Mark, He's the miraculous. In Luke, He's the Son of Man. In John, He's the Son of God. In Acts, He's redemption for the Gentiles. In Romans, He's my righteousness. In 1st and 2nd Corinthians, He's the uniter, He's the body and my faithfulness. In Galatians, He's redemption from the curse. In Ephesians, He's the head of the church. In Philippians, He's the God that supplies. In Colossians, He's the firstborn over all creation. In 1st and 2nd Thessalonians, He's my soon returning king. In 1st and 2nd Timothy, He is my mediator. In Titus, my faithful pastor. In Philemon, He prepares a room for me in my father's house. In Hebrews, my faithful priest. In James, He is the great physician. In 1 Peter, He is the incorruptible seed. In 2 Peter, He's my divine nature. In the Johns, He is love. In Jude, He keeps me from falling. And in the book of Revelation, from His mouth comes a sword, and written on His thigh is the name King of Kings and Lord of Lords.

To Adam, He was the creator. To Abel, He was the sacrifice. To Noah, He was a rainbow. To Abraham, He was a ram in the thicket. To Isaac, He was the well at Rehoboth. To Jacob, He was the rock at Bethel. To Joseph, He was the dream-giver. To Samson, He was the Lehi River. To David, He was a sword, but to Solomon, He was rest. And to you and me, He's our defense and He's our witness and He's our reward. He is our double portion and He is our faithful provider. He is the mighty one of Israel, the rose of Sharon, the lily of the field, my rock and my shepherd.

And all of this is just the tip of the iceberg. If you want to find yourself, dig.

Keep digging into Jesus. It is not me who lives, but Christ who lives in me.

Chapter 4
I AM Who?

How are you to become who you were created to be? There are three simple truths we have revealed so far. The first, transformation happens by revealing who Christ is, since He is the one living in me. The second truth, is that I am not my soul or my flesh. I am a spirit, born of Christ. My soul and flesh don't always have great ideas or insights, and they both like to be in control, but they are not me. Truth number three, is that Jesus is a warrior. I believe that we, as believers, have had a strength famine. We have been operating in defeat, because we operate from a place of weakness. When you come at a problem from a place of weakness you are not the warrior that Jesus is. The reason being is that we have not revealed the warrior side of Jesus. We have revealed a Jesus that is compassionate. He is meek, He turns the other cheek, and He is the Lamb of God Jesus. And this Jesus is needed. But, we have failed to reveal Jesus as a lion, a warrior, who from His mouth comes a sword, and His eyes are fire. He's ripped with muscles, and He's tough. On His leg is tattooed the phrase, 'King of Kings and Lord of Lords,' and He leads the armies of God on a white horse. What battles did Jesus fight? He fought with sickness, death, and the kingdom of darkness.

I John 3:2 (NKJV) *Beloved, now we are children of God; and it has not yet been revealed what we shall be, but we know that when He is revealed, we shall be like Him, for we shall see Him as He is.*

In other words, I will know who I am when Christ is revealed. Why? It says right here, for I will be like Him. When Christ is revealed in His many facets, then I too am revealed. This is my authentic self. In this chapter we focus on a fourth truth as we become who we are designed to be. This truth is found in the simple phrase "I am." If someone asks who you are, you might start with, "I am (insert your name)," and then a short description about what you do.

I was praying for a man one time, and we had an interesting conversation. He said, "Yeah, I just wanna see if God can heal my back or not." I said, "I know He can, but let's just see, man." He went on to say, "You talk about healing all the time, let's see if He can heal my back." I thought to myself, all right, I'm game, so I started praying for his back. I saw him look at his girlfriend with a face that was saying, "Whatever." I almost saw an eye roll. He was testing the whole thing, and I liked it. I thought, cool, he's a tough guy. I like a good fight. My Jesus wouldn't turn away from a battle. I began to pray. I asked him, "Move your back around, is it any better?" "No, it's not any better," he replied. "All right, thanks for trying, man," he said to me. I said, "No, no, I ain't done." Christians sometimes quit too early. It didn't work; you prayed for five minutes. Stop that! Just keep fighting. Who fights a war for five minutes? We have to be willing to get in it for the long haul. If it didn't work, keep fighting, keep praying, keep believing, and keep standing. I'll never give up on God's Word of Truth. "Come back here," I said. "What?" He replied. "Come back here, I'm not done praying for you until that thing starts to change!" I continued to pray. People around me started questioning what I was doing. I was not done praying yet. I had to push in more. My God is real, and His word is true, and this man was going to give it a bigger effort, or at least some effort. So, I prayed for him again; nothing happened. Prayed for him again; nothing happened. Fifteen minutes of praying later, "Do you feel something?" I asked. "No, I don't feel nothing," he replied.

I explained, "I want you to give this a chance. For just a moment I want you to believe that Jesus can heal you. Do you believe? Now, you are going feel God come upon you. Are you ready? I'm going to pray for you, and you're going to feel God come upon you. Healing wants to be received but you have to believe it, brother. Are you a fighter? I don't get the idea you are fighting. Come on, get in the game, bro. I'll pray for you again. Now, you have to move your back around. Move it around, I want that pain to go away." He was an athlete. I wanted to see that pain go away. We have to keep fighting! Fifteen minutes is still not a very long fight. We could go years. It's okay to stand and fight for years. You can do it! Another few minutes pass. Now, maybe, it has been twenty minutes, I can't be sure, but it was a long time. Then he says, "Now that's weird. Yeah, I don't know man, that's weird. Hey, baby, come here, check this out." His girlfriend says, "What, what?" He says, "This is weird but it really is better. Hey, thank you, man!" Now some won't receive because of this reason or that, maybe doubt, but the Holy Spirit wouldn't let me just throw in the towel on this brother. The Holy Spirit was teaching me to listen to special instructions. I just needed to inspire this man to get in the fight.

We cannot give up so easy. Keep fighting. Even if it doesn't seem to be working, fight. Keep fighting. Stop operating from a place of weakness. Stop operating from a place of failure, and recognize that God is able. Jesus is on the inside of us, and He is power. Now, Jesus never fought with sinners. He loved the sinners. Right? He never blogged about all the sinners. "You need to change, you bunch of sinners!" He never posted on

Facebook, "You guys are sinners and you're all going to hell." People don't go to hell because they sin, did you know that? That's not why they go to hell. They go to hell because they don't believe in Jesus. They don't have the saving knowledge of Jesus Christ. Jesus fought the teachers of the Law. Why? Because the Law will increase sin, and it is a failed philosophy. When you teach the law, you increase sin. When you teach the Gospel of Jesus Christ, you increase forgiveness. Which one do you want? We want forgiveness to be taught. We want the lost to be saved.

I want to show you another story about our warrior Jesus and how He fights. The story is told in John 18. Jesus was about to be crucified. He spent the night praying and sweating blood in the Garden of Gethsemane, and now He and the disciples are on the move again. As we look at this story, I want to focus on the fact that Jesus is a warrior, and His weapon of choice is the mouth. They came to arrest Jesus with soldiers and torches, and Jesus knew it, so the Bible says:

> John 18:4-6 (NKJV) *Jesus therefore, knowing all things that would come upon Him, went forward and said to them, "Whom are you seeking? "They answered Him, "Jesus of Nazareth." Jesus said to them, "I am He." And Judas, who betrayed Him, also stood with them. Now when He said to them, "I am He," they drew back and fell to the ground.*

First, note that Jesus isn't running from a good fight. He went forward. In other words, here is this angry mob with torches and weapons coming to get Jesus, and He walked at them. Jesus was not afraid. Then He showed His power in a demonstration of words, because when He spoke, those who had come to arrest them were knocked on their backs. That is a healthy dose of awesomeness. Why did Jesus make such a display? Because he wanted us all to see that no one can take His life, but He gave His life. He wanted to show us a demonstration of His power.

Now, let's look at the words He used. They are important. Jesus said to them, "I am He." He didn't actually say, "I am He," in the Greek. He actually said, "I AM!" twice. It is in the imperative form, which means an exclamation point. "I AM! I AM!" The word, "He," is added by translators to help make sense in our ears. The translators also don't put it in twice. He said, "Ego eimi," in the Greek. That's like saying, "I AM, I AM!" So, really He said, "I AM that I AM!" At that phrase, what happened to the soldiers and the people who came to arrest him? They got knocked down. The power came from the words.

In this story, we see a contrasting weapon of choice. Peter is going to try to use his actual sword to protect Jesus.

John 18:10-11 (NKJV) *Then Simon Peter, having a sword, drew it and struck the high priest's servant, and cut off his right ear. The servant's name was Malchus. So Jesus said to Peter, "Put your sword into the sheath.*

Jesus is not okay with that kind of weapon. He's like, "NO! Wrong choice, Peter!" Why is this? It is because His weapon of choice is your mouth. His weapon of choice to defeat the power of darkness on this planet is your mouth. Christ wants to defeat the enemy, and He needs access to your lips. He needs you to submit your mouth to His will. Stop saying the wrong kind of stuff, and start saying what Jesus says.

Now, let's return to John chapter 8. We visited this story earlier in the book. The Pharisees wanted to kill somebody named Jesus. They questioned Jesus, "Who are you?" Remember, the "who am I" is revealed by figuring out who Christ is.

They are asking Him this question, "Who are you?" Jesus was saying, "You have to know where I'm from and where I'm going to know who I am."

> John 8:12 (ESV) *Jesus said, "I am the light of the world. Whoever follows me will not walk in darkness, but will have the light of life."*

Now, when He said, "I am," He rattled some cages with this phrase. We miss it because we don't speak Koine Greek and aren't Pharisees. We miss something important that happened in this moment. In Exodus 3, God visits Moses by a burning bush. He says to Moses (I'm paraphrasing), "I want you to take the people of Israel out of slavery in Egypt, to a land I will show you; a land that is flowing with milk and honey." Moses responds to God's call on his life the same way you and I would have, "Who am I?" Moses says this phrase, "Who am I that I should go to Pharaoh?"

Exodus 3:11-12 (NIV) *But Moses said to God, "Who am I that I should go to Pharaoh and bring the Israelites out of Egypt?" And God said, "I will be with you.*

God's response to 'who am I,' is "I'll be with you." Can you hear him saying it now? We say, "Who am I?" God is replying to you, "Who you are is defined in Me and my partnership with you." Who you are comes from God Almighty. Do you think you are the result of your past, Moses? A lot of times we define each other by what we've done. "Oh, that is Ted, he was a real estate broker for 10 years with his wife, but they divorced. Now he's in marketing." Moses has a past though. Remember, Moses, the guy you murdered 40 years ago? That's what Moses did. He murdered an Egyptian! You think who you are is defined by what you have done? Moses, you were the shepherd for the priest of Midian. You would think that God would respond, "Well, you're Moses, you're the shepherd for the Priest of Midian, born into the Egyptian palace but killed a man when you were forty and have been on the run ever since." But, God needed him to access a different source to define who he was! So, He said (paraphrased), "I'll be with you." Moses, you are going to figure out who you are in God Almighty. Why? It is because you were actually made in MY likeness and image. I'll be your identity. I'll tell you who you are, because I created you. Do not say, "I can't talk!" I gave you your mouth! I know you better than you know yourself."

For us it's defined a bit differently. When we ask, "Who am I?" Christ says, "I am in you." God wasn't in Moses, He was with Moses. But Christ is in us. The same Spirit that raised Christ from the dead dwells in me. I was crucified in Christ, nevertheless I live, yet not I, but Christ that lives in me. You are born of an incorruptible seed. Christ is in you. You ask, "Who am I?" Jesus says, "I am in you."

Moses then asked the question that we would ask, "Well then, who are you?" God responds with something very interesting. Exodus 3:14(NIV) God said to Moses, "I am who I am." Now, the Hebrew word here for 'who' can actually be translated a lot of different ways. For instance, your version of the Bible may say, "I Am that, I Am." What He says in Hebrew is, "a'hayah asher a'haya." Now, "haya" is the same word that God used when he said, "Be," in the phrase, "Let there be light." He actually said, "BE LIGHT." So, you could say he told Moses, "I BE that I BE." We translate it: I AM that I AM. The word "asher" translated here is, "that," or "who," and is a very unique word. It is a relative pronoun that can mean any number and any gender. It is all things. It was like He was saying, "I am all of everything you will ever need. If you need faith, I am faith. If you need love, I am love. I am Spirit, I Am."

So, let's say you're Moses. You're talking with the Israelites saying, "Hey, I'm here. I got sent here to help you." So, they say, "Well, who sent you?" "I Am sent me!" Moses replies. See how it ties together when I say, "I Am sent me?" It's as though there's a partnership happening. God is with me, therefore I am, because He is. He says, "I Am that. I Be that." When God says, "Be holy as I am holy," the interpretation of some will be that you need to "do" the holiness, if you want to be holy. That is not what God said. When God said, "Be holy," He declared holiness into you. Then He says, "Now act like you actually are." Do you see the difference? He makes me holy, which empowers me to behave differently. Just as He declared light. He called something that was not as though it were. When He looks at you and you say, "I'm not holy," you are wrong. You are holy, because He declared you holy. "I'm just a sinner," you may say. Guess what? He declared you holy. Guess what? You're a saint. Because He said it. Therefore, it must be! Praise God.

"Hayah asher hayah," has in it the phrase "hayah asher." When you see these two words, "hayah asher," put together in the Hebrew Bible, it is most commonly translated, "And it came to pass." The phrase of the declaration is also the result. I am what? Insert a word. Make sure it is in agreement with who Christ is, and it will come to pass. Why? It is because you are who Christ is. Moses was dealing with his capacity. He did not believe he was worthy to deal with Pharaoh, or to have this calling on his life. God is showing Moses that his capacity is going to be based upon God's power. Who you are, Moses, is going to be identified in who "I AM." This is also true with you and I. It is Christ in us who identifies who we are. When I say, "I am," I'm speaking on behalf of who Christ is. I am speaking who Christ is within me. Let the weak say I am strong. I am strong because I have the I AM (Christ) residing on the inside of me. If I say, "I am not that smart," or, "I am broke," then I have forgotten who I Am really is.

Now, let's tie the Hebrew and Greek together here. Three hundred years before Christ was born, seventy Hebrew scholars got together and wrote the Septuagint. The Septuagint is the first five books of the Bible translated into Koine Greek. Koine Greek was the common Greek language of the time. The Hebrews were translating the Bible from Hebrew to Greek. When they translated this conversation between God and Moses, and got to this exact sentence where God said "I AM that I AM," the translation they came up with in the Greek is, "Ego eimi." It means, I Am that I Am. They created a phrase you would not normally use in common language or in a common sentence, "Ego eimi." Jesus and the teachers of the Law would've been familiar with this term as a most holy and set apart name of God. When Jesus said, "I am the light of the world," He used the phrase, "Ego eimi." He was not supposed to do that. That was a huge no-no. He used the phrase that God calls Himself.

Jesus uses this same phrase in the Gospel of John 8 as He is attempting to reveal who He is.

John 8:23 (NIV) ...*You are from below; I am from above. You are of this world; I am not of this world."* (Bold added for emphasis)

He used the phrase, "Ego eimi." I Am. He knew Who He was. He was using the phrase that the Pharisees attributed to God alone, from the conversation God had with Moses. He was being bold like a lion, confident in Who He is. The problem with many of us believers is we don't know who we are. We say who we are, but we don't come into agreement with the "I Am" residing within us. "I Am," is here and He's in you. He's who you are, but when you don't come into agreement with who He is, there's no power. "I am not that smart. I am crippled and broken. I am an addict!" We say things about ourselves because we don't realize who we truly are. When we are not in agreement with who Christ is, we cripple our own authority.

The other day I had some coffee cake. Have you ever had coffee cake before? It's cinnamon-cakey goodness. Know what it doesn't taste like? It doesn't taste anything like coffee. For the first 40 years of my life I didn't have coffee cake for one simple reason, I didn't want cake that tasted like coffee. People would ask, "Would you like coffee cake?" I was like, "No, I don't want coffee cake. Why would you want to eat cake that tastes like coffee?" That's like eating carrot cake. You don't take something that tastes bad and make a cake out of it! Raspberry cake would be good. Strawberry cake would be great. Then one day I realized that coffee cake doesn't taste like coffee, but it is a cake that you eat with your coffee; hence the name, coffee cake. Terrible name. That would be like strawberry cake with no strawberries in it. You would be like, "Where's the strawberries?" You find out, no, this is a cake that you eat with your strawberries. That doesn't even make sense! Who is naming the coffee cake? Horrible name. I missed out on 40 years of pure, cinnamon sugary goodness because somebody named it wrong. Coffee cake does not know who it is! It is having an identity crisis. It needs to be called cinnamon goodness or something like that. That would be a great name, AND people would eat it! Ha!

In the same way, you have named yourself incorrectly, and you have lost the power of who you are. You describe yourself by your weakness, but your I am is not in agreement with that. Therefore, you are not in agreement with yourself. What you need to do is learn how to say, "I am," and recognize that when you say, "I am," you are speaking who Christ is. We operate out of a place of weakness in our lives because we have failed to speak who Christ is in us. He's the 'I Am that I Am.'

If I met you and said, "Hi, I'm Pastor Jason and I am the light of this world."

What would your reaction be? "I am the light of this world." Would it rub you a little weird? Say it out loud right now. Say, "I am the light of this world." You say it. It feels funny, doesn't it? When you say it you're like, "Ummm... I'm not sure. I don't know if that feels right, Pastor. That felt funny." That's because you're operating out of a place of weakness, and you've been lied to about who you are. We are so afraid of being courageous and brave. We have been put under a false pretense of humility by people in the church and the world. And now we have forgotten who we are.

It was Christ who said in Matthew 5:14 (NET) "YOU are the light of this world." Yet, when you say it, you feel funny. Why? The reason is because you have been lied to, and now you operate out of a place of weakness. Jesus said it about you, and you're afraid to say it about yourself. It is because the enemy has lied to us Christians to keep us weak. When you declare, 'I am,' you are coming into agreement with who Christ is within you. That IS who you are. You have to speak in agreement with who Christ says that you are.

Jesus continues to reveal himself through the same Greek "Ego eimi," saying, "I AM," over and over again in the same sacred fashion that God introduced Himself to Moses.

John 8:24(NASB) *Therefore I said unto you that you will die in your sins, for unless you believe that I am He you will die in your sins.*

Jesus says, "I AM," in John 8:24. The translators have added a "He" in it. It should read: *Therefore I said unto you that you will die in your sins, for unless you believe that I AM you will die in your sins.* "He," is not there. In the Greek, it's not there. Translators have added it into our modern Scripture so that it sounds more natural. Now let us wrap this thing up as Jesus did, with a big bang. Jesus is leading up to His "drop the mic" moment.

> John 8:52-59 (NET) *Then the Judeans responded, "Now we know you're possessed by a demon! Both Abraham and the prophets died, and yet you say, 'If anyone obeys my teaching, he will never experience death.' You aren't greater than our father Abraham who died, are you? And the prophets died too! Who do you claim to be?" Jesus replied, "If I glorify myself, my glory is worthless. The one who glorifies me is my Father, about whom you people say, 'He is our God.' Yet you do not know him, but I know him. If I were to say that I do not know him, I would be a liar like you. But I do know him, and I obey his teaching. Your father Abraham was overjoyed to see my day, and he saw it and was glad." Then the Jews said to Him, "You are not yet fifty years old, and have You seen Abraham?"*

Drum roll please...vs. 58...

> *Jesus said to them, "I tell you the solemn truth, before Abraham came into existence, **I am!**" Then they picked up stones to throw at him.*

Oh, BOOM! It's going down for real, right? Just in case they had missed His reference over and over again to God's identification to Moses, "*I AM that I AM,*" Jesus makes it perfectly clear what He is saying. This would have been the "drop the mic" moment. Remember, the translators have just put the "I Am" in there once, but he actually says it twice in the Greek. He says, "I AM that I AM." This was a stone-able offense. This is our bold as a lion Jesus. Do you have this boldness in you? You do! Consider how God reveals this to us as a personal confession. When we say "I AM" we are assigning Christ to ourselves.

I am in covenant with the living God. I am the righteousness of God. I am filled with the same Spirit that raised Christ from the dead. I am transformed into the likeness and image of Christ. I am crucified with Christ. I am resurrected with Christ. I am alive in Christ. I am created in Christ. I am complete in Christ.

Now understand this: when you say, "I am," you are harmonizing with who Christ is. I am, because He is. Jesus said to the soldiers, "Who are you looking for?" And they replied, "We are looking for Jesus of Nazareth." He said, "I AM that I AM," and they fell down. There is power in *that* I AM. When you say, "I AM," who you are comes into agreement with who He AM (is). Praise God!

When you speak it, you now have that power within you. Say this aloud: "I am heir of the world. I am free of sin. I am free from death. I am free from the curse. I am free from fear. I am the branches. I am a son of God. I am righteous. I am sanctified. I am redeemed. I am holy. I am a saint. I am healed. I am delivered. I am fruitful. I am forgiven. I am saved. I am a king. I am a royal priesthood. I am a holy nation. I am blessed when I go in. I am blessed when I come out. I am the head. I am above. I am raised up and seated with Christ. I am strong." This is the authentic you, and when you say it, there is power. There is no power for victory in saying negative things about yourself.

Praise God! We have to bring who we are into agreement with who Christ is, and recognize who we really are.

Chapter 5

You are a New Creation

God has a calling and destiny for you. There is a reason why you were created. He has a destination for your life. But, in order to receive His destination for your life, you have to have a revelation of Christ in you. Why? Because God is going to give you things to do that you cannot do without His creative power manifesting in your life. He's already called you to do things that you will not be able to attain to without Him. He has put a journey in front of you that requires

His power to get you there. Let's explore the manifestation power of Christ in our life by looking at who we have become. The two are completely related. In this chapter we are going to really dive into this idea that you are a new creation. I've been saying it all along, but now it is really time for us to explore this concept and make it part of our identity.

> 2 Corinthians 5:17 (NKJV) *Therefore, if anyone is in Christ, he is a new creation; old things have passed away; behold, all things have become new.*

I like the word "behold" in this Scripture. It's like, "Woohoo! Party!" Behold (woohoo, yay, party-time) all things have become new.

The word "become," in the Greek, is in the past tense form. Many Christians are trying to "become" someone. Instead, they need to discover who they already *have* become. In 1 Kings 12:3-5, there's a story about a young man named Rehoboam. I encourage you to read through it. Here's my paraphrase: Rehoboam had just become king, and he was trying to figure out who he was going to become as a king. His dad was Solomon. His grandpa was King David. Rehoboam had some big shoes to try and fill. As the son of Solomon he succeeded him and became king of Israel. People approached him and asked him what kind of king he would be. Would he be like his father?

The people and the whole assembly of Israel went to Rehoboam, and said, "Your father put a heavy yoke on us. But now, lighten the harsh labor and the heavy yoke he put on us and we will serve you." Rehoboam answered, "Go away for three days and then come back to me." So the people went away. Rehoboam first went to the elders, those who had served his father, and those leaders who served Solomon. He said, "What should I do about this?" He was asking because he was trying to figure out who he would become. "What kind of king will I be?"

Are we asking ourselves this question in our lives? What kind of Christian will I be? What kind of husband will I be this year? What kind of wife or mother will I be? What kind of person, employee, or leader will I be?

Rehoboam was asking the question, "Who will I become?" He approached the elders and inquired, "What do you think?" They said, "If you will serve the people and give them a kind answer, they will be your people and serve you all their lives."

He went to some of his young buddies, the guys he grew up with, and he asked them, "What do you guys think that I should do?" And they said, "We think you should be tougher. You should be a strong leader." Tell the people, "If you thought my dad's yoke was heavy, my little finger is even heavier than all of my dad." Tell them, "Maybe my dad scourged you with whips, but I'm going to scourge you with scorpions." He listened to the buddies, and gave attention to their advice, and he became that sort of king.

He went to the Israelite people and said the same thing. He said, "You thought my father was tough, I'm going to be even tougher. I'm going to scourge you with scorpions." This response actually made matters much worse. Rehoboam listened to the wrong voices in his life, and the result was a great rebellion. The Bible says that at that time, a different guy named Jeroboam, who was one of the men there, led a great rebellion and the kingdom of Israel was divided.

Did you know that Israel went through a period of what we call the Divided Kingdom, where Judah was a different nation than Israel? This is when that moment happened. This is the moment of that rebellion, and that Divided Kingdom was established under this reign.

Rehoboam gave attention to the wrong voice of who he would become. If you feel in your life you've been operating at half capacity, maybe the reason is because you've been giving the attention to the wrong voices. Did you know that you will become like the voices you are listening to? When we get around the wrong kind of people they will influence who we become.

Jesus does things differently. With Jesus, He will be the one inside of you. Jesus will be the voice telling you who you're becoming. He says, *"I will never leave you nor forsake you,"* (Hebrews 13:5 NKJV). If you're going to become who you're around, you might as well be around Jesus. When you get around the right voice, Jesus' voice, instead of operating life at half capacity, you begin to operate in the double portion. This is what God has for you. We don't desire half, we desire double of God's promises.

Who have you become? Let's now look at the passage just above our revelation that we are a new creation. What was Paul talking about leading up to this passage? He starts off with "*The love of Christ compels us...* (2 Corinthians 5:14 NKJV). You are compelled by the love of Christ. When you became born again,

Christ's love took authority and influence in your life. The reason you attend church is because the love of Christ compels you. Before you knew Christ, church was not an every week event for you. His love compelled you to wake up and get into His house. The reason you want to do what's right in your life and make good decisions, is because the love of Christ is compelling you. You didn't used to care that much about right and wrong, but the flesh went after what it wanted. Now the love of Christ compels our hearts. Let's continue on with the passage.

> 2 Corinthians 5:14-15 (NKJV) *For the love of Christ compels us, because we judge thus: that if One died for all, then all died; and He died for all, that those who live should live no longer for themselves, but for Him who died for them and rose again.*

The moment you received Jesus into your heart, the old you died. The person that you had been, the one born of the flesh, it perished the moment you became born again. As a born again Christian you live for Jesus, the One who died for you. Before you were born again, you lived for yourself. You did whatever you wanted to do. Life was all about you. Now that you are born again, you don't live for yourself any more. You live now to produce fruit and to love God. You are living for Him who died for you and rose again.

Your flesh is full of failures and weaknesses. God wants to shed that former way of living. Let's continue on in this same passage.

2 Corinthians 5:16 (NKJV) *Therefore, from now on, we regard no one according to the flesh. Even though we have known Christ according to the flesh, yet now we know Him thus no longer.*

Why? It is because you are going to be serving and producing for God now. He wants to shed you of your flesh, which is full of failures and weaknesses. This is accomplished by getting Christ's power to manifest in your life.

First and foremost, we have to take our flesh out of the equation. The flesh just doesn't matter. Even Jesus said, *"The flesh counts for nothing."* (John 6:63 NIV) Life is not about the flesh and its desires. You have to let go of the flesh. You're not going to do this by your own works *or* by your own strength.

Let me show you something. Christians like to say, "If Jesus can live sinless, so can I. He was in the flesh. He was man and He lived a sinless life. So, I'm going to live a sinless life like He did." Don't make this about your effort. Take hold of your mind and fix your thoughts on spiritual things. If we want to see Christ manifest miraculous power in our lives, we have to forget about the flesh. There is a greater power in the unseen world than in the physical world. Can we just let the flesh go for a second? The flesh died when you became born again. Which means that now you are born of the spirit. You weren't rebirthed as flesh, but you were born as spirit. Adam was a breathing soul but Jesus was a life-giving Spirit. (1 Corinthians 15:45 NASB)

What did Jesus say in the Garden of Gethsemane? *"The spirit is willing but the flesh is weak."* (Matthew 26:41 NIV) Why do you want to operate in weakness? Just let it go.

Now here comes the window of power. I need you to serve and produce for God. Let's get rid of the weakness and let's move into the strength and power that God has for you. Here it is all together:

2 Corinthians 5:16-17 (NKJV) *Therefore, from now on, we regard no one according to the flesh. Even though we have known Christ according to the flesh, yet now we know Him thus no longer. Therefore, if anyone is in Christ, he is a new creation; old things have passed away; behold, all things have become new.*

It says, "All things." How many is all? All things have become new. You aren't trying to *become*. You aren't trying to change. *You're done*. In this world, we are trained in behavior modification. Behavior modification will change your identification, who you are. The premise being, if I just change my behavior, it will change who I am. The quest, though, is not to change your behavior. That's the old quest. The Old Covenant was: you are a bad, wicked person so here are the rules to change you. It was behavior modification. Change your behavior and then you'll be good. We learned however that the Old Covenant didn't work. That process is broken; it's not going to work. We've got to let it go.

The quest, though, is not to change your behavior. My quest is to see Christ manifest in my life, to discover Him in who I have become. My quest isn't trying to change me; my quest is simply to discover me.

We are all trying to change ourselves. That's what we do; we are trained to change each other. I've got to change you. I can change my boss, and I can change my wife. The reality is people hate change. We change our address, we change what car we drive, and we change our oil. We change our pool water, we change our shampoo, and we change our eating habits. We are constantly changing stuff. We try and change our spouse. Husbands try and change wives. Wives try and change husbands. You find out you can't wear that with that anymore. You used to be able to dress yourself when you were dating! You dressed yourself just fine. But now, you get married and find out that you cannot dress yourself. "Where are the comfortable sweats I used to have?" Long pause. "Oh, I don't know. I haven't seen those in a while," she says.

Yeah, she threw them away. Let it go. I went to get on the scale the other day. I noticed my wife looking at me, so I sucked in my belly a little bit and stood up a little taller. She said, "That's not going to change anything." I said, "Sure, it does. Now I can see the numbers."

My watch is even trying to change me. It tries to tell me to get up and breathe. I don't know if you have one of these fitness watches, but they try and tell you what to do. I have enough stuff trying to control me without a piece of electronics telling me to walk more. Are you serious? Now you're in on it, trying to change me? It said to me the other day, "You need to breathe." I began to fight with my watch. I'm like, "Man, you don't even know me. I've been breathing since I woke up. I haven't stopped breathing."

I want to emphasize to you, we are not trying to change ourselves here, and instead, we're trying to get a revelation of who we have become. If we get a revelation of who Christ is in us and who we have become, then our behavior will change into who we are now. Look, it's quite simple. Don't try and change who you are. Instead, discover Christ in you.

You're not trying to change the addict, right? That's what the world says, "We got to stop being addicted. Let's change your addiction." You're not trying to change the addiction; you're simply trying to realize that *you are not addicted*. The old you was addicted, but that person is dead and gone, and now you have become a new creation in Christ. God didn't create you as an addict. He created you completely set free, a finished work in Christ. You just have to realize, "I'm not addicted." The goal now becomes: to discover who I am in the world.

If you go to AA, Alcoholics Anonymous, they will create accountability for your actions, which is good, but then they're going to try and keep you in it. You have heard, "Hi, my name is Ted and I'm an alcoholic." Even though you're abstaining, "I haven't had a drink for two years but I'm an alcoholic." No, you're not an *alcoholic*. The world's philosophy says you will always be an alcoholic. They label you. But, this is not who you are. *All things have become new* (2 Corinthians 5:17 NKJV). The old you was an addict and an alcoholic, but that's passed away. Stop digging up that old grave! You have been set free! Praise God!

> 2 Corinthians 3:18 (NKJV) *But we all, with unveiled face, beholding as in a mirror the glory of the Lord, are being transformed into the same image from glory to glory, just as by the Spirit of the Lord.*

Here it says we are being transformed into the image of the glory of the Christ. The transformation process has been misunderstood by many Christians. The process of transformation isn't through changing a behavior, but rather, it's through revealing who Christ is in you. In other words, as I behold the glory of the Lord, I am being transformed. The mirror I am looking into is the Word of God, and it reveals Christ, of whom I am a reflection. What many Christians try and do is change their behavior so they can act more like Christ. Instead, we want to discover and reveal who you have become that is already Christ-like. In the transformation, you're not trying to act like Christ, you're trying to realize that you are made Christ-like. You can't make yourself Christ-like. It is God who made you Christ-like.

The Bible says that, *"I am complete in Him."* (Colossians 2:10). Jesus didn't finish half the work. He finished all the work. He completed you in Him. You are already complete. The job now is learning to unravel who you are *not* anymore.

The power of Christ manifesting in your life begins to be revealed as Christ is revealed. The manifestation of Christ will start with identification. He has made you complete in Him. In fact, you already have His mind. You have the mind of Christ. You have His power. You have His abilities. You have His purpose. You have His plan. You have His holiness, and you have His righteousness. He has made you complete in Him. Say, "*I am complete.*"

You are a completed work. He didn't forget to finish. If you have some area in your life that is not experiencing the manifestation of Christ, maybe an introduction is needed?

I've got to introduce Christ to my lack. Lack needs to have an introduction to my new identification. Here's a conversation that I would have with my lack, because my lack has been talking to me for years:

Me: "Hi, lack. How have you been doing?"

Lack: "Yeah, pretty good. I mean, we're a little short this week but I'm good."

Me: "Listen, lack, you've been telling me what to say and talking to me for years. You're always up in my business, telling me that we don't have enough money, and that we're short on cash, and I keep repeating what you say. I keep saying what you say. I don't have enough money to pay the bills. We can't do this and we can't do that. I'm not sure that we are able to give. We are shackled by our debts."

We live in and we listen to the voice called lack in our lives. Maybe lack needs an introduction to Jesus. Because Jesus is in me and I might need to say, "Hey, lack, I want to introduce you to a friend of mine. I know you haven't met him yet but this is Jesus. And Jesus, this is lack. Now, lack, you might want to run because Jesus is not going to be okay with you." Jesus, He starts rolling up His sleeves. He's like, "I'm going to deal with you right now, buddy. Listen to me, lack, come here. I got up on a cross and died so that you wouldn't be here anymore. I became poor that you might be rich. You need to go."

Maybe your lack just hasn't heard about Jesus in your life. Maybe your sorrow just needs an introduction: "Hey, sorrow. I'd like you to meet the Prince of Peace. Come talk to Jesus right now because He's got some words for you." An introduction to our identification becomes necessary.

So, let us look at a statement that Jesus makes about our identification. We are going to look at Luke chapter 10 now. We start in verse 19.

Jesus said, *"Behold, I give you the authority to trample on serpents and scorpions, and over all, the power over the enemy..."* (Luke 10:19 NKJV). You are going to trample it, you are going to walk on it, you are going to be the one with the power to overtake the enemy. When everyone else is terrified and petrified, you're going to do the electric slide, because your Jesus was crucified, and you're being glorified. In fact, you've been Jesus-fied. I hope that's a word.

Jesus goes on to say, *"Nothing shall by any means, hurt you,"* (Luke 10:19 NKJV). This word *hurt* means to injure you. Nothing is going to injure you, by any means. There are many "means" of being hurt, but none of them will work. Satan has no power over you, and nothing's going to hurt you. Nothing is going to hurt who you are, and nothing is going to hurt who you have become. When God created you, the new you He created... it is invincible. Remember? Incorruptible. The new you He created, that has become, is born of God, not born of this world, and therefore, cannot be harmed. The new you is incapable of going through a healing process, since the new you is already healed. God created you invincible and incapable of being injured. The old you still has sorrow, defeat, brokenness, and gets his feelings hurt, but the new you is, and I'm gonna make up a word right now, "uninjurable".

Satan wants to mold who you are through injury. He wants to change who you are to get you off course. He wants to keep you from seeing God's manifest power in your life by keeping you injured and down. The reason you stay in your sorrow is because you keep listening to sorrow from the past, which lies to your future. If you're still dealing with a sorrow, it's because it's lying to you. Don't listen to it anymore, it's just telling you lies.

Jesus says, "You're not going to get hurt anymore." Are you tired of getting hurt? God doesn't have hurt for you. God created a way in which you no longer have to be hurt.

Jesus continues this conversation with His disciples in the next verse as He says, *"Nevertheless do not rejoice in this, that the spirits are subject to you, but rather rejoice because your names are written in heaven,"* (Luke 10:20 NKJV). Jesus was showing everyone that the spirits being subject to you is not *the big deal*. He's like, "It's not even worth rejoicing over." So what's the big deal?

Jesus says, "Don't be all psyched up because demons are afraid of you, but rather rejoice because your names are written in heaven." The name being written in heaven is the big deal! So, He is saying that your identification is married to your authorization. In other words, your identity is married to your authority. He was saying, "I'm actually talking about the names. You're going to have authority over all, because I wrote your name in heaven. I have identified you in the heavens."

Think about that. When you have a driver's license, it's your identification and it gives you the authority to drive a car. Think about your name written in heaven. What kind of authority does it give you on this planet? Those things that are in heaven should be on earth, and you can call it out. Lord, make it like heaven in my life today.

I once went to a Kansas City Chiefs' Christmas party. I got to meet all of the football players and they signed a hat for me. Joe Montana was there and Neil Smith was there. Marcus Allen was there. Praise God, it was some of the greatest football players in the world that year. The reason I got in was because a friend of mine played for the Chiefs and he got my name on the list. This man was such a giver, such an amazing person, and a crazy good football player too. His authority was used to put me on the list so I could attend. So, all I had to do was show up with my identification and say, "Yeah, I should be on the list," and then they let me in. You see, my identification was married to the authority, or my authorization. In the same way, your new identity is married to your authority. If you're operating without authority, it is probably because you're operating on the old identification. You're operating out of the old flesh. You've got to find out your new identity in Christ and who you have become. You are a completed work.

In 1902, a man named Willis Carrier was standing on a platform waiting for a train in Pittsburgh when he saw the fog rolling in. He suddenly had an idea. He was an engineer and he thought, "I could cool air and dry it at the same time, the same way I'm seeing what's happening here in nature." Willis Carrier invented the air conditioner. When he presented the air conditioner in 1902, he said, "Here's the air conditioner." The people reacted, "What is that?" The first thing people want is the identification.

Kelli and I have had a few children. When you have a new baby, and the new baby is born, it is a new creation. This baby wasn't here before, and is a one of a kind. What did God say about you? He said, "Anyone who is in Christ is a new creation," (2 Corinthians 5:17 NKJV). So, you are a new creation. You are born again. A long time ago, you were born of flesh and blood, but when you received Jesus into your heart, you became born again. In fact, that's when the old person died and the new person was born. Now you are a new creation in Christ. When our son Matthew was born, he was a brand new baby. He never existed before. He was a new creation. There was nobody like him. He had his own abilities, his own talents, his own potential, his own plans, and his own destiny. When he arrived they asked, "What do you want to name him?" We wanted to name him Matthew. So, I went to the thing and I filled out a little card: Mathew Anderson. Kelli was in the room recovering, so I went to fill out the birth certificate information. I filled out the card: Mathew Patrick Anderson. Months later, we received the birth certificate in the mail. My wife opened it and exclaimed, "They spelled his name wrong!" I said, "What are you talking about? Let me look at that." I snatched it from her hand. "That's spelled right." I said. And she replies, "Is that how you spelled it?" I defended myself, "Yeah, that's how I filled it out." She said, "That's not how you spell Matthew. Matthew has two T's." I said, "No, it doesn't." She said, "Yes, it does."

I said, "Look, I spelled it the way it is in the Bible. I'm sure God doesn't spell it wrong." She said, "Go get me a Bible." Oops. She was right. Two T's. I spelled my son's name wrong. What's my point? You maybe spelled *your* name wrong, but now God has written your name down and says to you, as Christ is, so also are you. Your authorization is married to your identification. The problem is that you keep forgetting who you have become, you keep misspelling your name, and you keep operating out of who you used to be. So, you are operating without authority. You speak to that mountain but it just stares at you.

Once you have an identification of a new creation, it then needs an operation. The air conditioner that Willis Carrier invented had to be turned on. When it turned on, it began to operate. When it moved in its operation, it manifested into its destination. It began to do what it was designed and purposed to do. It never did what it was designed and purposed to do until it was turned on. But, how many of you know that Willis Carrier completed the work *before he ever turned it on*? That new creation was completed when He introduced it. In just the same way, God has completed the work in you! Here's a new creation. It's complete in Christ. It's you, and it's being introduced to this world. Now, you have to begin to operate according to your new identification.

It's an "air conditioner," so it's designed to cool air. It can't fix cars. That's not what it was designed to do. It's designed to cool air. In the same way, you have a new identification; you can't do what you used to do. Now, you have a new operation; allow Christ to operate through you because He's in you. The quest to see Christ manifest is by identification and to realize the operation of Christ in you.

> James 1:23-24 (NIV) *Anyone who listens to the word but does not do what it says is like someone who looks at his face in a mirror and, after looking at himself, goes away and immediately forgets what he looks like.*

When you hear the Word of God you are seeing a reflection of yourself. You hear the word and you see who you have become: completed work. You have everything inside of you, all power and all authority. You have the Spirit of God dwelling in you, and you have a New Covenant with the Creator of heaven and earth. You are brother/sister to Christ and your father is Father God. Lord Jesus, how could you possibly lose?

When you hear the Word, you're like a person looking at their reflection in a mirror. You are seeing who you actually are. That's who you are. Jesus is the Word, and He lives in you. But, if you don't do what the Word says, you're like someone who looks at his face in a mirror and after looking, he goes away and immediately forgets what he looks like.

The reason we're not behaving Christ-like is because we keep forgetting what we look like. You keep acting like the old dude instead of realizing who you have become. You're listening to the Word of God, and you're hearing the Word of God. What's God saying about you? You're thinking, "I don't know if I can do that." And God reminds you, "I can do *all things* through Christ who strengthens me."

"I'm being defeated right now, pastor." You are more than an overcomer in Christ Jesus. No weapon formed against you will win. Remember what you look like. That's what you have to do. Maybe your fear needs to look in the mirror. You say, "Fear, this is what the Bible says you look like." And you go, "Oh." You have no fear. Anyone who turns his eyes to Jesus, as the veil falls off of his eyes, begins to see who he actually is, and he knows the truth. And the truth shall set him free. (John 8:32 NIV)

When you stumble, it is because you forgot what you look like. Every time you blow it, you end in defeat, or you have some sort of failure in your life, you just forgot who you were. *You* actually didn't fail, the old you did. I said it before and I'll say it again. We cannot change ourselves by changing our behavior. We cannot change each other by changing behavior. All the wives out there, you're thinking, "Man, my husband. He's a mess. I've got to fix him." You can't fix him. My wife's been trying to fix me for years. Ask her, it didn't work. You can't change him. Husbands out there, you're like, "I need to fix my wife." You can't change your spouse. But when they (your spouse) hear the Word of God they actually see who they are. "My teen is out of control. My anger is getting worse." Whatever it is that needs more Christ has a simple solution. It needs to hear Christ. You, your teen, your spouse, your boss, they all need to hear Christ. Only in this will the authentic you show up. You will be transformed into the likeness of the Son, Jesus.

We don't need to try and change each other. What we need to do is spur one another on, more and more, to hearing the Word of God, and in that we remember who we are. If you want to speed up the transformation process in your life, or in the life of that teenaged son, then get under the Word of God. Reading is great, but this Scripture was trying to get you to the gathering place by only giving you the "hearing" option.

You want to see somebody transformed and become who they're actually called to be? If you want to see Christ manifest in a big way in your life, stop listening to who you used to be and start listening to who you are. Christ in you.

Chapter 6

Who AM I and What CAN I do?

The only voice that can produce the proper action in your life, is the voice of your Creator, God. If I am to imitate Christ, I need to know who Christ is. In this chapter, I want to take the puzzle pieces found in this book and put them altogether. We will be pulling on scripture we have already been looking at, but diving in more, to squeeze out that "aha" moment we all need. Let's start here with that mirror, the Word of God. It's about to show you who you are and what you can do.

> 2 Corinthians 3:18 (NKJV) *But we all, with unveiled face, beholding as in a mirror the glory of the Lord, are being transformed into the same image from glory to glory, just as by the Spirit of the Lord.*

The "unveiled face" is as if you had taken a blindfold off. Was I blindfolded? Yeah, you were. When the Word of God was heard, under the Old Covenant, it was like the people were blindfolded. Jesus said it this way, (paraphrased) "You're hearing but you're not understanding. You're hearing, but you're not perceiving." He said, "You're seeing but you're blind, and you're not perceiving with your sight." (Matthew 13:14-15 NIV)

The people would hear the Word, and yet, they did not understand it, or have a revelation of it. Without revelation there is no life, and there is no manifestation of the Word into our future. When *anyone* turns to Jesus, the veil is removed. This is what happens when you receive Jesus to be the Lord of your life. Before you knew Jesus, you would read the Bible and get nothing out of it. You knew it was full of life, but it was mysterious. When you know Jesus, and you've turned your face to Jesus, the veil falls off. This is because we have received the Holy Spirit. He is our teacher now, and He speaks in the language of the New Covenant. Your ability to perceive the hidden mysteries, and wisdom of God, has been given to you. Every time you hear the Word of God you have the ability to tap into a revelation that will change your future. Praise God!

How important is it that we hear more and more Word? *"We all, with unveiled faces...beholding the glory of the Lord."* I love the word, *"beholding."* I'm not just looking at the Word, but I am beholding it. I am enthralled by it, surprised by it, and I'm captivated by it. I'm like, "Whoa! Look at that!" Our reaction when we're hearing the Word of God, "Whoa!" There's an announcement being made when "behold" is in the Word.

"Beholding as in a mirror..." What am I beholding? The Glory of the Lord. We are talking about Jesus here. Anyone who turns to the Lord, when he hears the Word, he turns to Jesus. He begins to behold the Glory of Christ. As you hear the Word of God, it paints an image of the Glory of Christ in your mind, in your heart, and in your spirit. That glory reveals you being transformed into the same image of Jesus, the image of the Glory of Jesus. As that image is being painted within you, the Word of God begins to reveal the glory of Jesus. This is the mirror. When you look at it, you begin to be transformed into the image of Jesus. Wow! Imagine if Christ got ahold of your marriage, or imagine if Christ got ahold of your job. Send Jesus to your job instead of

you. Imagine how successful Jesus would be running your business for one day. Imagine Jesus, who is not afraid of that mountain standing in the way. Jesus, who is not worried about sickness or death, and He is not worried about paying the bills. You put Jesus in your life and watch what He can do. When I hear the Word, I begin to manifest the image of Christ in me. This is who I actually am. A new creation needs to have a new identification. When I hear the Word, I see who I am now.

The Scripture goes on to say, the image of Christ's glory is transforming us into the *"same image from glory to glory..."* Why? Is it because there are so many facets of who Jesus is. Yes! There's *this* glory of Christ, and then there's *that* glory of Christ. Now you are saying, "There's that glory. Oh! And, there's Jesus there. Oh! *This is what Jesus is like,* and then, *that's what Jesus like!"* He is the lamb of my sacrifice. He's the lion, He's a warrior, and He's the Prince of Peace.

Boy, I could use a little peace right now. He's healing, He's the binder of the broken hearted, and He's my hallelujah. He's the praise of my glory, and He's the King of Kings. He's exactly what I need.

When we *hear* God's Word we want to also *do* God's Word.

James 1:22-24 (NKJV) *But be doers of the word, and not hearers only, deceiving yourselves. For if anyone is a hearer of the word and not a doer, he is like a man observing his natural face in a mirror; for he observes himself, goes away, and immediately forgets what kind of man he was.*

When you learn that you are a new creation in Christ, but don't operate in it, you are like a person who looked in the mirror, and as you walked away, you forgot what you looked like. So, you heard the teaching on Sunday. The Word told you "You can do all things through Christ who strengthens you." On Monday though, you went back to your fears. The Word of God came to you as you sat in the Sanctuary and said, "Be anxious for nothing, but in everything, by prayer and petition, with thanksgiving, present your requests to God." However, on Monday, you didn't pray, you returned back to the old you, you had a temper tantrum, and you got all moody again. Why? Because you forgot what you look like. You started to act like the old you, right? The *new* you has authority. The *new* you, has Satan under his feet. The old you, that you keep trying to operate in, does not have Satan under his feet. Stop operating in the old you! The *new* you, has the power of the Spirit! You don't pray over the sick; it's Christ in you that prays over the sick! This is something to get excited about! Because, *"Greater is He that is within me than he that is in the world."* (1 John 4:4 NKJV) The *new* you, according to the Word of God, is righteous. The *new* you is Holy. The new you is perfectly obedient, invincible from harm, and incorruptible, that's the new you. Why would you want to be the old you? Why would you want to go back to the old you? The old you, he's a mess. Stop digging up an old you! He's dead; leave him in the grave.

People say, "Well, I've always had a temper. I get angry really fast, it's just part of who I am. I am Irish." We tend to define ourselves by our genetics. Well, my mom was diabetic so I have diabetes. I have allergies, or I have a slow metabolism, or I'm not good with Math. You name it, people define themselves by traits or genetics. The boss comes to you with a new project, "Hey, check this out I got this project for you." It's an opportunity for promotion. They see something great in you, and the favor of God is on you. But out of your mouth is, "I'm not good with spreadsheets. I don't think I could do this." Are you kidding me? Is this how Jesus would talk? Jesus says, "I can walk on water and raise the dead, but computers, forget about it…" Maybe the old you wasn't good with spreadsheets, but the new you has the mind of Christ!

Would you start believing what God says about you?

Jesus was born on this planet. The Word became flesh and dwelt among us, and He walked in our shoes. The Book of Hebrews says, "We do not have a high priest who was unable to sympathize with our weaknesses." (Hebrews 4:15 NIV) He went through the same temptations and trials. He just did a much better job of it.

When Jesus was around 12 years old, the Bible says that his mother and father went to Jerusalem, and when they left, they forgot to take their son with them. I don't know how this happens, but I mean, come on, let's not judge people. Like, which one of us has never left their kid in Jerusalem before? We've all done it. After three days, Mary and Joseph returned to Jerusalem to find Jesus. Which is a long time for Jesus to be missing...but I'm not judging anyone.

Luke 2:46 (NKJV) *Now so it was that after three days they found Him in the temple, sitting in the midst of the teachers, both listening to them and asking them questions.*

I want you to see a cool prophesy here. We read that it was after three days they found him in the temple. It was also three days after Jesus' death, burial and resurrection that He ascended to the spiritual, heavenly temple and was seated next to our Heavenly Father. Here, in Jerusalem, his parents find Him sitting in the midst of the teachers. This prophecy shows us who Jesus is and where we find Him. He's sitting and resting. And, He wants us to enter His rest in the house of God. Jesus was sitting in the midst of the teachers, both listening to them and asking them questions. He is not playing video games like most 12-year-old kids would be doing! He was in the temple, talking to the professors. In Jerusalem, if these instructors were the A team, then they were the professionals of the time.

They were the NBA or the NFL of the teachers of the Law. There were teachers across Israel in many synagogues, but Jerusalem was like "The Big-Leagues." These were the best of the best instructors. We know they were wrong, and Jesus would bear that out later. I showed early in this book that Jesus was not professionally trained by the schools of the day. As they are listening to this kid talk in the Temple they said, "Who is this kid that knows the Bible so well?"

> Luke 2:47 (NKJV) *And all who heard Him were astonished at His understanding and answers.*

The best teachers of the Law, who knew the Scriptures better than everyone, were astonished by a 12-year-old! Jesus left with his parents, and the Bible says that He *"increased in wisdom and in stature..."* (Luke 2:52 NKJV) He increased in wisdom with God. If He increased in wisdom with God, that would mean He did not already have the maximum amount of wisdom at that time. This means Jesus wasn't born knowing all. He is God with us, but when He was born a man here, he got dealt the same cards you and I started with. He had to learn to walk, talk, and learn the Bible. *When Jesus was born, He faced and went through the same challenges of life that we go through.* I like the idea that maybe Jesus was born and knew everything. It's cool to think that He came into the world already talking, or maybe He was in the manger quoting Scripture. I love that idea, right? But, He wasn't, He had to learn the Word of God just like us.

When He was 30-years-old-ish, a heavenly interaction happens between Jesus and God. We do not have a heavenly interaction between God and Jesus recorded in the Bible before this moment. It wasn't like at 15-years-old God visited Him and said, "You are the Messiah, now keep reading that Bible." When Jesus was being baptized, God spoke, *"You are my Son, whom I love; with you I am well pleased."*(Luke 3:22 NIV)

Why am I showing you this? Because, for the first 30 years of His life, how did He KNOW that He was the Messiah? As far as the Bible has disclosed (it is a complete and finished work), God had not personally revealed this to Him until He was baptized. Therefore, He had to believe what his mom and dad told Him about Him being the Son of God. He would, of course, have had the inner witness of the Spirit telling Him, "Yes, what they're saying is true." (You would need that because everybody thinks that their kid is the Messiah, right?)

The Bible says that Jesus was in the Synagogue on the Sabbath every single week. This was His custom. (Luke 4:16 NIV) He went to the house of God and heard the Word of God. He had heard from His parents that He was the Messiah. But, He had to figure out how and what He had to do. He had to learn the steps and procedures. He would have been asking questions, "When do I start, how do I do this, and how do I accomplish what God has put in front of me?" His parents had told him, "You are the Messiah." Joseph would have been like, "Yeah, I'm your stand in daddy, but your real father is God. You're the Messiah." So, Jesus might have asked, "Well, what does the Messiah do? Who is He?" And where are the answers to these questions? This would explain why He would have been at church so much. He would hear about Himself every time He heard the Word of God, in God's house. *The teachers of the law were astonished at his knowledge and wisdom*. He was just a young boy, how did he know so much? I believe every time He read the Word or heard the Word, He was looking for His identity. "Who am I and what am I here to do?"

A lot of people read the Word wrong. They're reading the Word looking for what everybody else is supposed to be doing, or even stop doing. They read to find out what makes everyone else a sinner, and they end up placing a veil on their own eyes. When you turn to the Lord Jesus Christ, you begin to see the image of Christ. When you read the Word, you are looking for who am I in Christ, and what am I here to do?

After Jesus was baptized, He heard the word of the Lord speak out, "*You are my Son, whom I love; with you I am well pleased.*" Afterward, He went into the wilderness, He fasted for 40 days, and then He was tempted by Satan. What was He doing? He was operating in His identity. My point, God was saying to Jesus: this is who you are, (paraphrased) "*you are my Son, and you're right on track, keep going.*"

When Jesus heard the voice of the Lord, He stepped into operating in His purpose. You see, the Bible does not say that He operated in the power of the Spirit when He was a carpenter. He was not operating in divine power when He was making shelves and entertainment centers for His neighbors, although, I'm certain they were great. See, He went out fasting and came back in the power of the Spirit. This is what we want in our lives. I want Christ to manifest in your week, in relationships, and in your business.

Jesus walked out fasting, but when He returned, He had the power of the Spirit on Him! Jesus was about to stir it up! He was about to raise the dead! No more making end tables and stools. He was about to heal some sick, and bind some broken hearted. Oh! Snap! He was about to raise up a crippled man! He was about to give sight to a blind man. He's about to change some things on this planet!

Up until He was the age of 30, we can see in Scripture, He didn't operate in the power of the Spirit. I can say that with confidence, because of what it says about Him returning in the power of the Spirit. That was new for Him. But now, He had the power. He had an identification moment when He heard the voice of God. This is My Son with whom I'm well-pleased. And, He began to operate in His identity.

The same goes for you today. The voice of God is speaking to you today; you are God's son or daughter. You are a child of God. Don't think for a second that God is not well-pleased with you. He is well-pleased with you, because He is pleased by your faith in Jesus Christ. Somebody might say, "There is no way God is pleased with me." Oh! Yes, He is! Because you are the righteousness of God created in Christ. God has declared you Holy and blameless. He washed you white as snow. You may say, "But, I'm a mess." No, you're not. The old creation of you was a mess, but now, you are a new creation in Christ Jesus. God did not create a mess. He created you fabulous.

Jesus returned to his hometown of Galilee, and when He did, He returned with the power of the Spirit. In the same way, we need to return to our Galilee in the power of the Spirit.

Galilee was Jesus' home town. When He went back to His home town, the Galileans remembered him differently. They spoke a different definition of who He was. The home town said, "Isn't this just that Jesus guy? Didn't that guy make me a shoe closet last year or something? Who is this? Why is he preaching the Word of God and praying over people?" But Jesus chose not to listen to the voices around him. He wouldn't allow them to define His identity. We should apply this same thinking for ourselves. When you get to your hometown tomorrow, don't allow the voices around you to define who you are. Don't allow your friends, family, co-workers, and relatives to define who you are! Even Jesus' family tried to re-define Him. When you are in your Galilee, don't believe those voices. You're going to believe the voice of God! Say, "I'm a child of God. I'm moving in the mighty miraculous power." If you want to see the supernatural in your life, you've got to begin to operate in the realm of the supernatural. I'm not going to believe the voices in my Galilee; I'm going to believe in the voice of my Creator.

The news of Jesus went throughout all the surrounding regions. Look, there's going to be chatter about you when you begin walking in the power of God! With power He created you to operate in, people are going to start talking about you. Your name will be on the lips of your co-workers and your friends. "What's gotten into Ted? Man, Ted used to be kind of timid and weak and he didn't do anything. He was kind of a loser. He didn't seem very smart and he'd never take on new projects. But, Ted seems different now. What has gotten into Ted?" I'll tell you what's gotten into Ted. The Spirit of the living God started to manifest in Ted. Jesus was already in there, but Ted started finally letting Him out. Ted was able to do this because he began to

169

recognize who he was in Christ, and he started to operate in that position.

What is this and how does it operate? I think too many Christians are having what I would call an identity crisis. They are operating as Christ in one moment, and then they slip back into their old identity in the second moment. It is like being a divided person.

My son Christian's car is a 1988 IROC Z28. It's an awesome, manly car. Sometimes I drive it. Oh, man, that car can go! Other times, I will drive my daughter's car. Her car is a very, very little, yellow, kind of wimpy car, if I could say that. It's roughly the size of one of those plastic balls you put a hamster in. And, it's not like a masculine yellow color. It's a feminine yellow. Depending on what I'm doing that day, I will tend to drive either one of those cars. When you drive the IROC Z28, it's a masculine powered, 350 cubic inches, 5.7 liter, fuel injected, tuned, ported, dual exhaust,

4.11 gear ratio, positraction with 50's on the back. When you start it up, you can hear it from two blocks away. When you sit in that car your muscles just get bigger without working out. You know what I mean? You just sit down, and suddenly you're manlier. I shaved before heading out the other day. As I sat down in the IROC to leave, boom, whiskers came out of my face! And, when you drive the IROC, you have to put the window down and arm out across the door. So cool. Are you feeling it? Now, when you drive my daughter's car, it has its own unique identity. In fact, for me, I'm kind of hiding in it. The other day I found myself checking my nails. "Oh! I should get a pedicure and a manicure!" What am I thinking?? I'm a man! What am I doing? I'm having a crisis here! When you get out of my son's IROC Z28, you have to strut. You get out of that car and you have to slam the big heavy steel door with two hands, then you widen your stance and walk slowly, as you glare at anyone nearby. You get out of my daughter's car and you kind of hide behind your hands, as you slink into the nearest shadow, thinking, "I hope no one saw me driving that. I hope no one's looking at me right now. 'I'm valeting for somebody else. I'm just a valet, just dropping this off. Errrr uhhh, It's my daughter's.'"

How many of us are forgetting who we are in Christ? Have we forgotten how much strength we have in Him? He's the IROC, loaded with power. We are overcomers; we can strut with the power of God in us, confident, full of courage, and ready for any challenge. So many Christians act like they're driving the little wimpy car. But, if we will begin to look, as James says, into the perfect law of liberty, it will set us free. What is the *perfect law of liberty*? It means to be perfectly set free and it's a law. It's just like the law of gravity. If you jump out of an airplane without a parachute, you're in trouble, you're going to fall. The perfect law of liberty says, "You are set free because of who you are in Christ." You can pretend you still have prison clothes on, you can pretend like the shackles are still on, but you have been set free, and it's a law. And anyone who looks in the perfect law of liberty begins to see, "I'm not who I used to be. I'm not that person anymore." We are not who we use to be. Before Jesus, we were of the defeated, but now we are champions. We looked into that perfect law of liberty, and we found out that we used to be broken, but, now, we are whole. We were of the sick, but now we are the healed. You run into somebody who has known you from Galilee and they're like, "I remember you." And you reply, "Yes, I used to be a different guy. I used to be blind, I used to be lost, I used to be enslaved to this body and whatever it wanted to do. I used to be shackled in the prison of my genetics. I was behind the bars of my sorrows. I was jailed and held back by my past. But, praise God, Jesus has set me free. I am not who I used to be, and he who the Son set free is free indeed. I am of the mighty, I am of the prosperous, and I am covered with favor."

You are victorious in Christ. Start acting as God created you to be, and operate in that capacity.

On Christmas Eve, my brother was showing my dad this long staff that he gave him. It was a long metal staff. He began taking it apart. I went over to see what they were doing, and he pulled something out, and now there was a spear on one end. They pulled out the tube of the spear, and now it's like a saw. Then he unscrewed a little section of the saw, and he pulled out what looked like to be a little axe that you could chop wood with. The axe head pops off and he pulled out a lighter. I was so confused1 I was like, "What is that?" When we see something new we have questions.

It was a prototype my brother was working on. So, I asked him, "What is it? What does it do?" These are the normal questions we ask when we see a new creation. I had never seen it before. And these are the right questions. Again,

"What is it? What does it do?" Who we ask matters. If had asked my wife, in the next room, she maybe could have guessed, or just said she didn't know. I was asking the correct person because my brother was the creator. It's the same for us. You are a new creation. Are you asking the right person who you are and what you can do? Or, are you listening to the wrong voices? We must ask our creator, who we are, and what we are here to do.

I was on a tour playing a concert in Reno, Nevada. The venue was an underground theatre. At the end of the night, we were loading up our gear in an elevator. We loaded the heavy speakers and equipment on this elevator. It was a freight elevator and I had never been on one before. I didn't understand how it operated. Now, I know how normal elevators operate, but this was a bit different. As the elevator was closing, a door came down from the top, like a garage door, which I know what that looks like. I say, "Oh! It's like a garage door elevator or something." As it started closing from the top, I realized I'd left something on the stage, and I decided to jump out of the elevator. As I looked at the garage door coming down, I gauged the speed to make sure that I could get underneath the door. I decided to, as I stared at it, duck underneath and climb on out. But, as I ducked underneath it, what I did not realize was that another door was coming up from the ground at the same time. BAM! My head hit that bottom door so hard. When I hit that thing, I was like, "Oh! Lord." And, I placed my hand, with a lot of pressure, right above my eyebrow. Blood began dripping and running down my arm. I had split my head open right above my eyebrow. I had to go to the hospital that night, and the band, of course, went to Denny's. Because that's what men do.

Band: "So, you're going to get some stitches? Alright. We're going to go get some pancakes. We'll see you in a little bit?"

Me: "Yes, thanks guys."

So, I got 15 stitches across my eyebrow, and then wore a beanie the rest of the tour, because I looked like Frankenstein. What's my point? If we don't know how something operates, we can sometimes get injured. God knows how you operate. He knows how creation operates. He has all the information you need to make sure you stop cracking your head open as you move through this life.

We get married and we think, "I'll just do the things my mom and dad did in their marriage. Or, I'll ask my buddy. Or, maybe I'll listen to Hollywood, since it's going so well for them." And what happens is ... we crack open our head on our marriage. Our intentions are to have a great marriage. But, we need to get the right information from the Creator.

When I was younger, I would meet up to workout with three other guys. One guy was an accountant, the others were lawyers. We would meet up at 5:00am at a fitness center. All these guys were married, and I had just gotten married, and they would talk about their marriages. They would try and give me advice. They would say, "Oh! You just got married. Let me give you my philosophy. Here's how you do this, and here's how you do that." I realized, as a very young man, they didn't even like their wives. Why would I want to listen to their philosophy about marriage? So, I decided to go to the Bible to find out about marriage. The Bible said, "Husbands love your wives as Christ loved the church and gave himself up for her." So, I thought, "Okay. That's how I will operate. I have Christ in me, and Christ is happiest when he's doing what He likes to do. He likes to sacrifice himself for his wife, his bride." I've heard people say, "I don't really like the church." Well, Jesus loves His church. If you're saying you don't like the church then guess what? You're talking out of your old man. Because, Christ in you, He is in love with the Church. And, if I come into agreement with what Christ says, watch out. There's something about Christ in me that is attracted to the church. Christ is in love with His bride, the Church. As a young married man, I began to operate as a man who would love his wife and lay down his life for her. My workout buddies, they had really bad ideas for how marriage works. I found out that Jesus had a different way. I found out that if you'll die to what you want, you'll get the life that Jesus has for you, where you will find complete happiness and fulfillment. When I learned how Christ operated, I got Jesus' results working in my marriage.

In Judges Chapter 6, Gideon was visited by God. An angel of the Lord comes to speak to him. The Bible says that Gideon was threshing wheat in a winepress. God's about to make a great ruler out of him, but Gideon thought, (paraphrased) "I'm weak. I'm the least of my clan, my clan is the least in the tribe, and my tribe is the least in all of Israel.

We are the lowest of the low, and I'm the lowest of them." At that moment, Gideon was a "nobody." No one knew who Gideon was. He was hiding in a winepress, threshing wheat. The Bible says it was because he was afraid. An angel visits him and says this, "The Lord is with you, mighty man of valor." Okay, Gideon didn't believe he was a mighty man of valor, but God knew he actually was. God knew something about him that he did not know about himself. Gideon did not believe this about himself, and therefore, was unable to operate in it. But, when God identified him as a mighty warrior, it gave him the ability to start operating like a mighty warrior.

And, without him stepping into the operation of mighty warrior, he would not have been able to set the Israelites free from the hand of the Midianites. If he didn't begin to operate as God described him, he wouldn't have had the victory, and his name wouldn't be in the Bible. When God identified him as a warrior, he began to operate as a warrior. You may not believe what God says about you, but God is right and you're wrong because He created you. And, today He is saying to you, "The Lord is with you mighty man (woman) of valor." You say, "I didn't know I was mighty, but okay. I am mighty, and I'm not going to be defined anymore by my oppressors, the Midianites." Let's choose today to not be defined by others anymore. I'm not going to be defined anymore by being the least in my clan. I'm going to listen to what God says about me, starting right now, and I'm going to start to operate in what He says. I know that God is about to do something great. I used to be blind, I used to be lost, and I used to be the least in my clan. What was he doing? He was threshing wheat in a wine press. That doesn't even make sense. When we're afraid, we don't make sense.

Gideon lost his identity. This is the picture of threshing wheat in a winepress. He was not using the winepress in its designed operation. The creator had an identity for it, but it is as though Gideon didn't understand that identity. The creator would say, "What are you doing? That is not what I built a winepress to do." He was working hard at something that was not producing anything in his life. In fact, he was living in fear. If you've been doing things in your life that are not producing, it might be because you keep trying to thresh wheat in a winepress. The problem is you have the wrong identification. You thresh wheat on a threshing floor, you press wine in a winepress. I don't know what Gideon was getting by threshing wheat in a winepress, maybe wheat juice or something? It makes no sense! He wasn't able to access the power of the wheat, which represents the bread of God to us. Neither was he able to access the wine, which is the covenant and the power and the Spirit of God poured out on you.

He was not able to access the forgiveness, the redemption, or the power of the Word of God, because he was confused about who he was. If you have been operating from that place in your life, I'm here to tell you today that you have been set free, and God says to you, "You are a mighty man of valor." Now, look into the perfect law of liberty. Hear the Word of God, and see that Christ is within you. The old things will pass away and you'll start stepping into the new manifestations in your life. You will walk into your job and you will truly be more than an overcomer in Christ Jesus. No weapon formed against you will prosper, and you will walk by faith and not by sight, seeing what God has called you to be.

When you read or hear the Word, you are to be searching for your own identity and purpose, as you see Christ's identity and purpose. He is in you, and you are in Him. The answers to "Who am I, and what can I do," are entirely revealed in God's Word. You are Christ in you, and so you can do what He can do. *All things*

If you're reading this and you've never given your life to God, you can do it right now. In John chapter three is a story of a man who visited Jesus in the night and asked how a person can get eternal life. Jesus response is that *God so loved the world that He gave His one and only son that **whoever believes** in Him would not die but would have everlasting life*. You see it is about a choice to **believe**. It is not about what you do. If you want to give your life to the Lord right now just say this simple prayer and mean it. Mean it in your heart and you can be saved.

Dear Father God, I ask you to forgive me of all my sins, and ask you Jesus, come into my life, come in to my heart, be my Lord and my Savior, and baptize me in the Holy Spirit, in Jesus name, Amen.

If you said that for the first time, find a church. You were born again into the family of God; now go join that family, gather with the believers. The very key to the timing and speed of your growth will hinge entirely on you hearing the word of God in God's house. This is God's pattern. Six days a week you are out working, doing your thing, and one day a week you are in God's house. Six days you hear from the world who you aren't, what you can't have, and what you can't do. It's important that one day we hear who our creator says we are, what He says we can do, and what He says we can have. We get our heads put back on straight, get some hope stirred up, we are reminded to love and to forgive. Be in church; do not let Satan deceive you into thinking it just isn't important. It is. Church is the very Bride of Christ.

And I want you in the church where I preach. I do.

www.livingwordonline.com

Made in the USA
Las Vegas, NV
05 December 2020

12091555R00108